# An Identity Worth Keeping

## Finding Yourself After Childhood Trauma

Pauline Ocharo

**PAULINE OCHARO**

To my mum

Thank you mum for being the best mum I could ever ask for.

# Introduction

This book will discuss the mental effects of child sexual abuse, the trauma of it and how to overcome them. I share my story, what I've learned on this journey, how I overcame and how you can. I still can't believe how far I have come despite everything I have been through. Let this book be an encouragement for you that despite anything you go through, it can always get better. Also, before you read, I want to remind you that healing is possible. I didn't think I could ever recover from my childhood trauma and my family's betrayal. Yet, here I am, writing a book that shows it's possible. Remember, your journey isn't going to look like mine or anyone else's because we are all different. Just know that God's intentional about your life and your story, and He will help you in a way that is unique to your life.

# My story

My life drastically changed at about the age of 9. One of the reasons was that I had moved to a different country, leaving all the family I knew behind. Now, I had to live with people I never knew existed. Some I had only seen over the phone at least once or twice. One of these new strangers was my biological father. Moving from my home country was supposed to be a life-changing experience in the most positive way ever. It was meant to be a change for the better, but that wasn't the reality. In fact, it was quite the opposite.

At first, my innocence made me believe that my father was a great guy. He made me feel very welcome. He took me to see the amazing sights in London, and I believed he treated me in a more loving way than he did to the others. How I innocently looked at my father didn't last too long. At age 9, my biological father started sexually abusing me. The abuse happened for about 5 years. Every day looked the same to me, so the 5 years didn't feel like 5 years. I don't remember much of what happened in those years. But I vividly recall how it started. He made it look all innocent at first. He built my trust and made me believe that he was the best father in the world; then, he used that to his advantage.

The fear and shame I felt through the years helped me survive those dark moments. Now, looking back, I notice that there was a very big fine line between loving my father and fearing him. I realised that I was afraid of what he could have done, so I loved him to protect myself. I can't imagine how different my childhood would have been had I understood how horrible my life was then.

The sexual abuse, along with verbal and occasional physical abuse, hurt me deeply. I questioned what I did to have deserved all of that. All I did was try to be the best child, but that didn't seem like it was enough. If I'm being quite honest, I don't really remember being a child. After coming to London, my childhood automatically ended. Now, all I remember of my childhood is how I was trying to cope with the pain of the abuse. The silent tears I shed after the abuse. The hateful words I uttered to myself for something I couldn't stop. The isolation I felt in a house full of people. The random outburst of anger towards myself and the perpetrator.

Not living with my mum didn't make it any easier. It felt like I'd been thrown into a dark, abandoned pit to suffer alone. I didn't help myself much. I had too much self-hate towards myself. I hated myself for allowing this man to do what he did to me. I constantly blamed myself for his actions. Each day after the abuse, I would look in my mirror and promise myself and God that it wouldn't happen again. Every time I broke this promise, it felt like God hated me. The little innocent me always told herself, "All it takes is a no, and everything will stop." It looked so simple when I was telling myself that, but when it came to the moment, saying no was hard. I was utterly stuck. I didn't know the abuse wasn't in my control. I had convinced myself that I was the reason why it was happening.

Everything that happened to me each day killed my self-esteem. I felt like just a walking body with no value. I felt myself fading away bit by bit. Emptiness overwhelmed me, and before I knew it, I had lost the little girl I was. As years passed, my rage grew. Yet I couldn't say a word. The one person who was supposed to keep me safe inflicted the deepest wounds. It was like my protector was also my worst enemy.

It got to a point where I felt unsafe in my own body. It's one thing to feel unsafe in certain environments, but it's another thing to feel unsafe in your own body. It's being enemies with your shadow, yet you can't run away from it. Self-hate was something I really struggled with. His actions poisoned my self-image, making it hard to blame him for his actions. I was stuck in a loop of hating myself and taking the blame for things that weren't my fault. I felt filthy and dirty and wanted to spend the rest of my life hidden in a dark, cold hole, so I never get to feel myself again.

Nobody around me was aware of what I was going through. I was happy they didn't though. That spared me from the embarrassment and shame attached to what was happening behind closed doors. To avoid them finding out, I had to fake my personality most of the time to the point where I became perfect at doing it. Only experts like younger me can cry themselves to sleep. Then, they can go to school looking like the happiest people in the world. To fake this happiness meant that many things had to be swept under the carpet; a busy schedule allowed me to do this. I was always in school doing extra activities. It wasn't hard to forget what happened to me the night before. I grew desensitised, managing to forget my past for a while. The abuse was so frequent it became my twisted normal. It was a reality I no longer questioned. It was only when the abuse had stopped that I started feeling the effects of it.

I noticed I had been walking around with an invisible dark cloud. Not even the sunniest summer day could brighten my world. As a child, it was hard to understand what I was going through and why my mind felt so clouded and lost. As I got older and learned more about mental health. I began to question and become more aware that I wasn't okay.

It wasn't until the 2019 lock down that everything that I was hiding came at me out of nowhere. That year is when I discovered that my childhood was abusive. Everything that I had hidden under my little carpet came out. I felt attacked, lost, and confused. I thought I had forgotten everything, so I was shocked that all these feelings were resurfacing. I had managed to be 'happy' for so long, so why was everything happening now? I still can't explain what that felt like to this day.

I battled with my thoughts. Over time, negative thinking became a part of me. Panic attacks and anxiety attacks had become part of my daily routine too. I was completely detached from myself. This experience made me realise I needed to change something about myself. Sweeping things under the carpet wasn't working anymore. That's why I will always say thanks to 17-year-old me. She made me realise I didn't know myself. Who am I? Why am I like this? Why do I act this way? She made me ask questions I couldn't answer. That's when I realised I needed to discover her. To discover the girl who I was underneath all that trauma I was buried in.

What I did a couple of months after this did nothing but destroy me. For some reason, I thought confronting my father would help me. I had confronted him many times before, but every response I got tore my heart to pieces. When I would say, "I hate you for all you have done!" He would reply, "I can't believe you hate me. You have such a bad heart." I don't know what made me think that things would be different this time, but it was no surprise that I got similar responses. I gave up. I was constantly speaking to a brick wall. It baffled me how the person hurting me couldn't stop it even after speaking out many times.

## My healing journey

A year and a couple months later, I was chilling in my room. One of the church members messaged me to confirm if I still wanted to be baptised. The thing is, I previously wanted to be baptised two years ago. But, two years later, that decision had completely changed. I thought I was nowhere near ready to be baptised. I put a priority on my mental health and wanted to get my life together before that could happen.

An hour after he had messaged me, I decided to say yes. I was a people pleaser, so saying no was hard. A week or two later after this, the preparation for my baptism started. I did all the necessary bible studies in preparation for this big day.

The day finally came: September 25th. After the baptism, I felt relieved and excited to have finally done it. The mistake I made was that I had over-glamourised what life would be like after I got baptised. I imagined that everything would fix itself and it would be a happy ever after like some sort of fairy tale. I convinced myself that all it would take was a baptism to change my whole life. I was right but wrong at the same time.

The baptism marked a new beginning and the start of a journey, but for the journey to be a success, I needed to partner with God. This is when I concluded that I needed to seek God wholeheartedly. For once, I noticed I had the right weapon to fight the battles in my mind; I just didn't know how powerful that weapon was.

After I got baptised, I yearned to know who God really was. I became intentional about my relationship with Him, but I didn't know how to go about any of this. I started off by picking up my bible and reading the popular stories I've heard people talk about.

Reading the bible always taught me something new about God. By knowing Him, I slowly started finding who I was. The main focus at the beginning was getting to know God and finding out what role He had to play in my story. Over time, God showed me that He didn't just have a role to play in my story, but He was the author of my whole life. Now, the focus shifted from why the abuse had to happen to me to what I was going to do so I could see myself as the girl God sees.

If I'm being completely honest, there were days I lost hope completely. As much as I was learning more about myself, my life still felt stagnant. I wanted to be better so bad that any signs of me being in the same place made me so harsh on myself. One day, I would think things were getting better, but then the next day, I would still get panic attacks. The negative thoughts didn't stop. Sometimes, they got so bad that I even wanted to give up. What kept me going through these times was God's constant reassurance that everything would be fine. The reassurance wouldn't come in the form of angels falling from heaven and dancing in my room. That would be amazing, wouldn't it? It was simple things like seeing an encouraging quote on Instagram. Stumbling on a video on YouTube which resonated with how I was feeling at specific times. The sudden relief you get from these simple things is unexplainable.

God repeatedly showed me that he was more than capable of mending my broken pieces and making me whole. He met me at my most broken moments and showed me that I should trust Him with my life because He gave it to me. After many tears, betrayals, and heartbreaks, God changed me beyond my wildest imagination. He made life worth living.

He used my story to teach me more about myself and grow my character. Through learning about who God was, I got to learn who I was. With the training of my mind, I was able to see myself how God sees me. I was able to accept the fact that despite going through the traumatic chapter of my story, there was still beauty in my future life. I noticed that even in my loneliest moments, God was with me all along.

My past had become my identity. I wanted to cling to every emotion because letting go meant that I had let go of everything that happened to me. When I chose to let God into those parts of my life, He came in and changed everything about me. He gave me a love which I never thought I would receive. The purest form of love. He cherished me, made me feel worthy, and gave me an identity worth keeping.

I had been walking around with this dark cloud that made my whole world so gloomy and dull. But, you see, God took that away. He replaced it with His light. He replaced it with His vision for my life. He turned my life and showed me that there was more to life than the life I was living. He still has a purpose for me. He showed me what peace looked like and gave me peace so I could also know what it means to have peace, which surpasses all understanding. I could go on about what God has done, but we will be here for ages. My story just goes to show you what life can be when God is the main character.

I really struggled with letting go of the fact that I was sexually abused. I knew I needed to do it one day; otherwise, I would be weighed down for the rest of my life. I remember thinking, 'If I let go of this thing, then what happens? What do I get in return for letting go of this thing that I feel so entitled to carry?' To make a long story short, I had to get to a point where I became tired of being tired. I got to a point where I decided to give it all to God. I had carried this trauma for so long that it got to a point where I was like, God, let me give you this part of my story, and you do whatever you want with me. I didn't know what I wanted God to do in my life, but all I wanted was to be happy. That's it!

At times, it became frustrating when I wasn't happy immediately because I thought that all I wanted was to be happy. I wasn't asking for the whole world, so why was it taking so long? Now I see why it took time. God wasn't just trying to make me happy for a few months. He wasn't trying to give episodes of happiness. He was going to change my whole life. Quite literally. He was going to take me to a place mentally that I didn't think I'd ever get to. He was going to heal me from the trauma so much that I became unrecognisable. So it's not that He didn't want to make me happy straight away, but he was building me and making me unlearn everything trauma taught me. Ever since I let go and let God, He has changed my whole entire life. He's moulded me, mended all the broken pieces, and healed the wounds they created. God met me at a really dark, helpless place, and He took me to where He knew I belonged.

It's frustrating being in the same place for so many years, and it's worse when you feel like you will be there forever. I thought that my life was done at the age of 17. Little did I know it was only getting started. I say it all the time. If God is doing it for me, He will definitely do the same for you. Your story might not be the same as mine, but the good thing is God is still the same. The way He worked and is still working in my life, He can definitely work that thing for you, too.

**Why am I writing this book?**

Everything written in this book isn't just about my story but also about how God worked through everything so I can be free from my trauma. It's an encouragement that you still have access to that type of healing. Without Him, I wouldn't be writing this book. I would still be stuck somewhere more lost than ever. But you see, when I met Jesus, He picked me up and swept me off my feet with His love. I knew He intended more with my story. He gave me comfort through my trauma, so I can use that same comfort to encourage you that your story doesn't end with the trauma. My life before was horrible. But I'm humbled that it turned around so much that it outweighs my past struggles. I've learnt that when God does something, He does it big.

There were days I was so happy that God found me, but I wanted to praise him in secret and not share my story. I was so happy to keep the testimony to myself. But this wasn't God's intention for my life. He had you in mind when He was instructing me to write this book. I'm praying that this book will comfort you and help you see God differently. It will kick-start your journey to finding who God is to you. This book helps you find an identity worth keeping. It's a love letter to every person that there's still life after trauma.

God turned my wounds into scars, so you know He can heal yours, too. I'm not where I used to be, and that's because God brought me to a better place. A place I couldn't even imagine myself being at. He met me at my most broken moments; when I thought my life was over, He told me it was just getting started. It breaks my heart to see so many individuals go through what I did and feel what I felt for so long. Many are broken-hearted, lost hope, and feel their situation will be like that forever. Some are comfortable in their situation because that's all they have known. Depression, abuse, and loneliness are all they know. But I'm here to remind you that it doesn't have to be like that forever. It won't be like that forever because of God. He will give you peace that surpasses all understanding. God doesn't limit the healing He gives. If He could do it for me, He most definitely can do it for you.

# YOU AND TRAUMA

# Under the carpet I go

Sweeping my problems under the carpet was the easiest way out for me. It was a temporary shield that protected me from having to face my reality. It wasn't the best way of dealing with my problems. I would be lying if I said it didn't give me a lot of short-term comfort. Brushing off my reality and pretending my problems weren't there was my way of coping. Sooner or later, I knew I would reach a point where I would have to face everything I'd hidden under that carpet. The longer I swept, the more my issues grew. It was only a matter of time before the weight of my hidden troubles became too much to bear.

There are better ways of dealing with problems, but sweeping is the easiest and quickest. When life struggles become too much, you don't choose to sweep your problems. Rather, it is something you are forced to do to cope with the issues in your life. A lot of quick ease and temporary freedom is received from not having to deal with your problems when they come up. Sweeping your problems under the rug is one way to ease emotional pain. It helps you for the time being, but remember, anything that's too easy comes with a price.

**Methods of sweeping: Busyness**

Being busy is one of the most common ways of running away from feelings and problems. When you are busy, your focus is on so many different things that your problem is blurred out for the time you are busy. You can use a busy schedule to mask the things you are going through.

Many avoidants find themselves always claiming to be busy and having a lot happening in their lives. Not knowing, they subconsciously make themselves busy to avoid their feelings. It can look like everything is fine until the busyness stops. Removing the schedule reveals the mess that remains undealt with. That's why, when things slow down, you may feel restless. You might crave a moment to be busy and distracted again.

Ignoring problems and being too busy to confront them makes them worse over time. Neglected issues tend to escalate and pile up, becoming harder to handle and causing you more stress. A sign you have been suppressing is when you have random cry outbursts that aren't triggered by anything. The pain builds up as you run away from it. Your tears signal the unresolved hurt you have been running from. The further along you run, the more weight gets added.

Confronting old wounds becomes harder with time, but facing them will finally bring relief. There's comfort found in running away, but when it does stop, you are forced to confront the pain you fled. It's in the moments of stillness that whatever you were hiding from gets revealed. This leaves you to feel the raw emotions of the experience without being able to pinpoint where the emotions are coming from. The real reason lurks beneath hidden traumas that you have swept under your carpet.

## Personality and actions as evidence

When I was younger, I had a lot of friends, but my father never let me hang out at their houses. My friends had to come over if they wanted to see me anywhere other than school. Nine times out of ten, my room would be untidy when my friends came around. I didn't want them to think I was messy. I would shove my scattered clothes into my wardrobe and squeeze the rest of the mess under the bed before they came in. It didn't matter what the inside of the wardrobe looked like because my friends would only be seeing the outside. The idea of my friends thinking my room was tidy made me feel good. I felt even better because I didn't have to spend a lot of time tidying my room or folding my clothes. But I couldn't help but feel unsettled. I knew later on I'd have to deal with that mess by myself. It became such a habit that my wardrobe was too full after a couple of weeks. The clothes began to fall out. This proved I needed to fold those clothes and tidy up everything.

Cleaning a small pile of clothes under a bed or wardrobe is easy. But, it gets harder with a large pile. You get confused. You don't know where to start to get everything together. So, you decide to leave it. This scenario is the same with emotions and experiences. Hiding and not dealing with your emotions will eventually create a messy pileup. As your pile of emotions grows, they will spill out in your actions when undealt with. Your behaviour then serves as evidence that something which needs to be dealt with is piling up. If it's not dealt with over time, you will start to become what's on your mind.

Sometimes, experiences can be suppressed so much that they vanish from the conscious mind. Hiding things and avoiding some emotions will leave you numb. Numb to the pain you have faced and numb to everything else that will happen to you. It can get so serious to the point where you forget that you have been hiding things in the first place. When you suppress, it means you become numb to the pain and the experience in order to protect yourself. This numbness doesn't remove the pain but protects you from it for a short while. When the things hidden under the carpet start to slip out, the pain will be the first to come out. Now what you will have is intense emotions but nothing to attach the pain to. That's what suppression does. It hides the meaning or reasoning behind your behaviour.

**Pauline's story**

At 17, I realised I had been sweeping everything under the carpet since the abuse started. I had completely forgotten what happened to me. One random golden hour evening, as I sat in my room, I suddenly remembered that I had been abused. I found the thought shocking because I couldn't understand how I had managed to forget it for so long. At times, I doubted my memory. It took a while to register in my mind, but as time went by, it was clear that my mind wasn't playing games with me. My memories were so graphic and ugly they leave me thinking, 'Nah, that can't be true; there's no way that happened to me.' As time went by, all the emotions and pain and hurt I had been hiding started to liven up. It was in these moments that I started to feel the mental effects of this hidden trauma. Everything that had been swept under that little carpet came at me. There was no more space under there.

### Your brain power

Your subconscious holds 90% of your brain power, while your conscious holds only 10%. That is why you may tell yourself to do one thing. Be convinced you will do it. But, when the time comes, you do something else. Your 10% can make a decision. But, if your 90% isn't programmed to act on it, the 90% will overrule the 10%. Burying experiences and emotions as a way of coping means there's a big chance you will forget them. The impact of these events doesn't get lost, so you can have certain behaviour habits which are influenced by what's been forgotten.

Knowing the power of the subconscious mind is key to figuring out the reasons why you do what you do. Look for patterns in your actions and ask yourself why. Your conscious mind may make a decision, but the subconscious often overrides it. It holds your stored programming. Explore your past. Take some time to reflect on your experiences. This can help you understand your actions and choices better.

### Temporary comfort

Remember to take your time to process your past experiences and emotions. Address them gradually to avoid feeling overwhelmed when they flood at you all at once. Running away from what hurts by using quick fixes will only keep you stuck in the place you want to escape. The short-term solutions will work when you use them. But they will ruin you in the end. Sometimes, the pain is unbearable, and the solution is the easiest, most damaging. What you do to fill in the void only leaves you emptier than when you started.

Hiding and suppressing your pain gives you short, false comfort that avoids the root cause. The suppressed pain will always come back. To heal from your pain, you must recognise its presence and then confront it. Allow yourself to feel the pain and process any emotions associated with that pain. It's uncomfortable, but facing your pain helps you know yourself better. It also deepens your understanding of your experiences.

**What do addictions look like?**

You will be fed up at one point in your life. You will want to let go and work on yourself, but it will be hard to do so.

Your brain now knows that whenever you feel a certain way, there's something that can be done to relieve that. Over time, if you don't indulge in these things, your body starts itching for them.

Your mind is stuck on what worked before, so it's hard to change. Changing your ways takes real work to undo what's become second nature. Every time you give in to temptation, it gets a tighter grip. The more you do something you know you shouldn't, the harder it is to stop. As habits form, breaking free gets tougher. But here's the thing: every choice you make counts, and it affects what happens next. Each time, you are putting yourself in a worse place than when you started. What was once supposed to numb the pain for a short while ends up costing you your future.

Your brain is malleable, meaning it can adapt change and grow. This gives hope that you will never be stuck at the same point unless you choose to. For example, let's say you struggle with being alone, and because of that, you jump from relationship to relationship to avoid it. Overcoming this means teaching your brain to deal with loneliness by doing something fun alone so you can be comfortable with your own company. Addictions prove that you are running away from things and emotions you are afraid to face. The first part of solving your addiction is dealing with the root problem and facing the pain. You can stop indulging in something you are addicted to for a short while. But, not addressing the root issue means triggers can resurface old habits. Overcoming addiction isn't just about stopping what you do. It's about finding and fixing the root issue of the addiction. Once you do that, changing the behaviour becomes easier.

**Finding freedom from your addictions**

When overcoming addictions, the focus should be on the root cause of the addiction. You can never truly overcome your addictions if you only focus on stopping what you are doing. Addictions are surface-level representations of the core issue deep inside you.

When thinking about being free from addictions, what you should be doing is getting in and digging deep to find the core reason why you are addicted to whatever you are addicted to. Get to the bottom of your addiction. Take a hard look at yourself. What's really driving you to keep going back? You need to know this stuff to break the cycle. Once you understand why you're stuck, you'll see how to get out. The goal isn't to stop overindulgence. It's to heal from the experiences that caused it. Think of experiences and emotions as the roots of a tree and addictions as the branches. If you remove the root, the whole tree, including the branches, falls. When you fix the core issue, the addictions will fall. They won't be supported anymore.

Addictions start when you try to comfort yourself from a problem you don't want to face. The longer you hide from the problem, the more you rely on whatever comforts you. The addiction works. It relieves you of your problem so you keep going back to it. It is easier than trying to find a solution.

Ignoring a problem will make it resurface later. If not dealt with, it can create cycles of repeated issues. These could have been prevented if they were addressed earlier. The more you ignore a problem, the harder it becomes to deal with it.

Overcoming addictions means getting to the core of what you are running away from. That means that you have to first recognise and accept that you have been running away from the problem and that you do have a tendency to avoid or ignore your problems.

Be honest with yourself and accept the addiction may offer some relief. But, its comfort is more damaging in the long run. The brave part of this process is then going on and reflecting on what you do to avoid the problems you have. Addictions aren't as clear as you think, so this allows you to pinpoint what you run to when you are faced with certain problems. Sometimes, forgetting your problems means doing things you swore not to do. But you do them anyway because they bring you comfort. Addictions go beyond substances and can manifest themselves as emotional crutches, they can also look like repeatedly seeking solace in someone you should have released long ago. It can look like spending too much time scrolling on social media to forget your problems.

When you are faced with a certain problem, pay attention to the thoughts and emotions that arise from it. Study yourself and clock on any avoidance or discomfort which comes from having those emotions. Being aware means you can interrupt your actions and choose to respond a different way each time. Before you know it, you will have gotten to a point where you bravely face your problems and challenge your thoughts—embracing discomfort. It's uncomfortable, but facing your issues will lead to a better life. Your well-being should always be your priority. When you want to run away from your problems, think about the long-term cost. Evaluate whether it's worth it or not. That may motivate you to face and respond to your problems differently each time.

**The deception**

The enemy knows that Jesus is the way, the truth and the life, but he doesn't want you to know and believe that. The Bible says that Jesus has won all victory, but the enemy wants you to think otherwise. When you are in a bad mental state, he makes you question who God is and makes you doubt that God can truly work in your life. Sooner or later, if you don't resist him, you'll fall into his trap and dive deeper into things which keep you hungry.

Your journey would have been smoother if you had dealt with your problems as they came. However, not everyone has the support to deal with trauma. As you go on the journey of decluttering your carpet and overcoming any addictions, know that you aren't doing it alone. God is right there with you, by your side. Don't beat yourself up for what you did during survival mode. Don't beat yourself up for the choices you made when you were trying to survive. In those moments, it's easy to make mistakes. It's also easy to prioritise short-term gains over long-term consequences. Learn from the past, and don't use it to make your life harder. Regret only takes up time and energy that could be used to find the person you were always meant to be.

**Advice**

Working on your mental health is draining when you do it yourself. It's okay to rely on help from a therapist and trusted family and friends. You can't be your own healer when you are the one who needs healing. You can't mend your broken pieces when you are the broken piece. A battle can't be won with just one person, but with Jesus, everything is possible! He knows everything about you because He created you. Give Him a chance. Every heavy burden you have, you can give that to Him, and He will give you rest. He knows that you have problems that are too heavy to carry. He also knows that when you give them all to Him, He will provide you with rest which is unique to your situation. The rest Jesus offers is unique to each person. Everyone has their own battle. Everyone has their own unique story, so everyone will get a solution that is unique to that story.

# Last straw

When I was younger, I loved listening to this song called fighting temptations. There's a part of the song that says, 'I used to wake up some days and wish I'd stayed asleep. I went to bed on top of the world, but today, the world's on top of me.' This part of the song resonated with how I felt on so many mornings when I would wake up each day.

Waking up with this heavy feeling was exhausting. What made it worse was not knowing why it was there. Hearing this part of the song brought so much ease. I didn't know why I felt this way each morning. But I was happy that something could describe the indescribable feeling. It's annoying to feel sad and low but not understand why. It's even harder when you can't find the words to describe the feeling. As time passed, I grew tired of the feeling and wanted to know what I could do to get rid of it. Searching for a solution left me with no hope. I concluded that nothing would take the feeling away. So, the real answer was to end it all.

One summer evening, I was sitting in my room looking through the window facing the garden. I was wearing my favourite mustard bandeau dress; I don't quite remember what my hair was like that day. The skies were blue, with a small hint of clouds. The sun had started setting so it was the perfect golden hour sunset. As the sun moved, the houses across from me were bright whilst my house became shaded. A clear presentation of how I was feeling inside: living in a bright world yet having a dull soul. I admired the beautiful sky with envy, knowing my pale life could never compare to its beauty. No sun, no clear sky, no golden hour sunset could have changed my mind. I'd already decided this moment was going to be my last. I couldn't do it anymore. I really couldn't. I had battled for so many years, but it was all too much.

Now there I was, sitting on my grey-ish chair, reflecting on my whole life so far. At such a young age, I carried the weight of emotions and pain caused by the one who was supposed to protect me. The burden was too much to bear at that age. I didn't even know the true meaning of life, and darkness was already messing with my days. Hope was barely visible. I'd been through so much at an early age, so what made me think it would get better from here?

Reminiscing about my life, I noticed that the only positive memories I had were of the times I spent with my mom and sisters. That was a few years back, so how bad was life that the last time I had a genuine smile was a distant memory? Feelings of anger and hate rushed through my body, bringing me back to my reality. Now, the sun had completely set; there was no glimpse of light, just shade. The sky was covered with white clouds, and the night had started making an entrance slowly.

I was angry at my father for what he had done to me. I was also angry at those around me for not noticing it. Even with all that fury towards my father, the person I hated the most was myself. I felt like the abuse was happening because I allowed it. Part of me knew I couldn't stop it. But another part tried to convince me I could. So, I blamed myself for the abuse. It was at this moment I became my own worst enemy. I proceeded to prepare to do what I had planned. But that's when a slight, gentle breeze blew past me. My mind went blank; it felt like the thoughts I had were gone. They hadn't gone forever, but at that specific moment, they had all disappeared. The quick shift in my thoughts made me question if God did it or if it was just my bipolar moments again. To cut a long story short, I got off the seat and went to nap in my bed.

That day, I believed every feeling I had about myself. This day, I felt like no one cared about me. God removed this thought by comforting me with a gentle breeze. He showed me that even though it doesn't look like anyone cares about me, He cares about me. This moment could have easily been the worst moment not only for myself but for my family as well. God stepping in and giving me comfort showed me I could believe Him for everything. I believed because He doesn't only say He cares about me, but He showed it.

**The lead up to suicidal thoughts**

Suicidal thoughts are like a never-ending war in your mind. You're constantly fighting whether life is worth living. It's like two voices arguing in your head. One whispers, telling you to hold on a little longer, but the other shouts, convincing you to give up. Though the thoughts may not be constant, when they come they feel powerful. When all you want is peace, battling these thoughts can make it impossible to have a peaceful mind. When this fight exhausts you, you start to lose hope. Deep down, you don't want to leave the world but would instead want to be in a new world. In a happy and peaceful world, a place where your thoughts don't war against you.

**Being isolated**

Adam and Eve were the first people to be created on Earth. God put them in a beautiful garden. He also gave them instructions about what they could and couldn't eat in the garden they were placed in. They were told they could eat from every tree except for the tree in the middle of the garden. A serpent approached Eve and made her question the instruction given by God. Eve fell for the trick and ate from the tree she was told not to eat from. Later on, Adam also went and did the same thing. Before eating from this tree, they were naked, but once they had eaten from it, they became naked and ashamed.

The enemy allured them to sin, and then once they did what the enemy had planned, he made them feel ashamed. He made them hide away from the presence of God so he could torment them with more of his lies. God saw that Adam had hidden himself, and asked him, 'Who told you are naked?' The simple answer was the devil.

The enemy is weak so his best tactic for keeping you in dark places is hiding you from the powerful one. He wants you isolated so he can make you believe you are not good enough and that life is not worth living. But God looks for you and asks you who told you all these lies because He didn't.

He knows what God says about you is powerful and true. But he doesn't want you to know that. Once he isolates you, you end up believing his lies about your life not being worthy of living. He hides you from seeing that God says you are valuable and that God will restore your life after trauma. When you are hidden, all you can see is what the devil presents to you, nothing else. This moment of isolation is a perfect time to torment you with life-sucking thoughts.

**Always waiting for an opportune time**

After fasting for 40 days, the devil tried to tempt Jesus. The devil tried to trick Jesus with lies. He failed because Jesus rebutted his lies by pointing back to what the word of God says.

The devil couldn't get to Jesus so he fled away but waited for another opportunity to try and tempt Jesus again. The tactic he used with Jesus is still the same one he uses today. The opposer will always wait for the right time. His power isn't strong enough to catch you at any time, so he must wait for a perfect time to capture your mind. He will wait for the moments when you show signs of defeat. He will wait till he sees you angry and losing patience with everything. He will wait until he sees you feeling extra insecure. He will wait for when you are getting triggered by past experiences. That's when he plants thoughts to heighten how you already feel. In weak moments like this, his power holds so much weight. Guess what though? God's strength is always made perfect in your weakness. When you feel weak and don't feel like you can pull through anymore, God strengthens you. That's why you find life has been a shambles for so long, but you still push. You still manage to do your day-to-day activities. You still manage to be a good friend, sister, mother, and father. That's only because even though you are tired, God is holding you up with His strength.

**Overcoming suicidal thoughts**

The first step is to acknowledge that the thoughts are there. You shouldn't try to hide or suppress them. The second step is to make sure that whenever you have these thoughts, you remind yourself of the truth about you.

Remind yourself about how God views you and what He says about your life and your future. God's thoughts are thoughts that give peace and life, so anything that doesn't do this isn't from Him. You gain power over your thoughts when you know only what God says needs to rule your life. Any other thought which doesn't match the truth about you can be eliminated or reduced by using God's word. For example, if your thoughts say you don't need to be here anymore and that life is pointless, shut them down. Reassure yourself that God is with you on this journey. When these thoughts appear in your mind, accept that they are there, but don't act on them.

Over time, this changes your mind. You now know the difference in your thoughts and the power they hold. By doing this, you teach yourself to know that God thinks of you more highly than the thoughts you have right now. Believing the facts about you won't be easy. This doesn't remove the truth from them though. The more you heal, the more you will accept the facts about yourself. The suicidal thoughts may have controlled your life. Now, it's time to give God a chance with the life He has given you. The devil wants to steal, kill, and destroy you. But God wants to give you a full abundant life.

**The thoughts God has towards you are thoughts of peace.**

Any negative thoughts including suicidal thoughts, don't come from God. The thoughts God has towards you are thoughts of peace and not evil. These thoughts give you a future and hope. Anything that ends life or makes you lose hope comes from the opposer. It is meant to discourage you. When your thoughts contradict God's words, just know that they are from the enemy. The opposer wants to push you to think about ending your life and eventually doing it. The devil knows that because of the great God you serve when you are healed, your story will do two things. It will testify to God's greatness. It will encourage others to know what God can do in their lives. He knows that once you start believing what God says about you, your life will be different in many ways. So, he aims to make you believe his lies so you don't see God's truth. The best way to know if a thought is from God or the enemy is by seeing and analysing what emotion it brings. Does it create life in you, or does it destroy it? Is the thought one that puts you back into a depressive state? The devil's ideas will always end life. It's clear. The bible says that the devil has come to steal. To steal your joy, to steal your peace, to steal your mind. He has come to kill. To kill every dream you have and everything that makes you burn with passion. To destroy you. To destroy you and deny you God's promises, to eliminate the life God would give you in abundance.

**You've made it this far for a reason.**

Remember that God didn't bring you this far to leave you. You have been through so much, but you are still here. That's because God still has a purpose for you. People will assume you are strong because you have made it this far against the odds. But the reason why you have managed to come this far isn't because you are strong. It's because God promises to always make a way for you. He will help you bear everything thrown at you. He will walk with you through it all. You may have gone through some things or may be going through them right now and you feel defeated. It feels like you can't get back up. But, you find a way to do your daily tasks. This is all because God is helping you; He's made a way for you to pull through it.

What you are going through right now cannot compare to what's going to happen after it. Even though what you are going through is so big. God will use that same exact thing to make you win. Joseph, a young man in the bible, was thrown into a pit by his brothers. His brothers had animosity against him, so when they threw him in, they intended for him to die. He had been sold as a slave, imprisoned, and falsely accused of sleeping with the king's wife. But years later, despite a hard life and many obstacles, Joseph became king and saved a nation. What was supposed to destroy him, God used to build him up.

Even though what you are going through is one of the worst experiences ever, please hang in there. What you are going through right now can't even come close to what is going to happen after. That's not to say you should neglect the feelings you are having now just because you know it gets better. Go through the process. Cry when you need to. Allow yourself to break down because to heal is to feel. While you feel your pain, feel it whilst knowing it's going to get better.

**It's not over**

I thought life would improve when the abuse from my father ended. I didn't realise that, with the abuse gone, the torment would start. I now felt the mental exhaustion of having to survive it.

Slowly, my life started feeling like it was over. I didn't know who I was or what was to come. I didn't think life could get worse, but as time went by, the misery increased. I didn't have hope that God could change my life the way he has changed it. The abuse affected every single part of my life. I can't even think of a part of my life which wasn't affected. I did have hope at certain times, but it was only minimal. I've only now realised that despite everything, God's blessing was bigger than my suffering. He is using what the devil wanted to destroy me to work out for my good. It's always easy to say this after God has changed your life, but it will be hard to see life past the trauma when you are in the process and on the journey. The pain and mental effects of abuse are life-changing. The pain you have to endure is one which can't even be wished on your worst enemy. But God still has a way of showing you that He is bigger than anything you will ever face. Even the things you feel are impossible to recover from are the exact things He will bring you out from. There's nothing you will ever face that He can't help you with.

# Identity Crisis

Your sense of self is built on memories and values but can easily fall apart. Your experiences shape who you are. But it can be hard to see what truly defines you when the identity of past experiences still shapes how you see yourself. It's confusing, and you are left searching for answers to what makes you who you are.

**Childhood and identity**

Having a carefree childhood is not just ideal—it's essential. The way you live in your childhood shapes your entire life. It decides how freely you live and cope in adulthood.

Things like abuse being in the presence of your childhood mess up your normal development. It takes you away from the path of normal childhood and diverts you into a path of survival mode. All of a sudden, you find that you have lost your innocent self and are forced to walk down a path you didn't choose. This kind of trauma can affect you for the rest of your life, leaving deep wounds that don't easily heal. The journey causes deep emotional trauma, leaving you mentally isolated and lost. You wished someone would come and save you. You dreamt about having a guide who can show you a new way, one that's not as painful as the path you walked in growing up.

If you were this child who did suffer the consequences of another's actions, you would know that abuse didn't just hinder your quest for identity. It also denied you the chance to have one.

Who you are right now is a result of what you have been through, not a reflection of who you truly are. That's why healing from childhood trauma means going on a journey to find what you never had. Your childhood was a painful, never-ending loop. So, healing isn't about re-discovering something you once had. It's you finding who you are for the first time. This makes the healing process confusing and frustrating. You don't know what to look for. All you know is that you want to be a better version of yourself, but you don't quite know what that will look like.

Starting your healing journey marks the beginning of discovering the person hidden under all that trauma. Finding you again means letting go of the false ideas trauma placed on you and getting ready to embrace the real you.

## The identity clash

What's not talked about enough is how hard it is to let go of trauma, especially when it has shaped who you are. It molds you into someone different, and letting go feels like losing a part of yourself. It's not as simple as moving on and forgetting about it. There's this ongoing tug-of-war inside you - part of you wants to let go, but another part feels like you're betraying a big part of your past if you do it. When trauma becomes deeply ingrained, letting it go is hard. It feels like you will lose a core part of yourself. You may become subconsciously resistant to help. It's not that you don't want it. It's that getting help means losing your current identity. Clinging to your past self yet wanting to let go and embrace a new identity can make healing look impossible.

It even becomes hard to imagine life past who you are right now. There comes a clash between who you are right now versus who you will become when you choose to let go. To ease your journey, release who trauma made you because that identity is not worth keeping. Be ready to embrace the girl you were meant to be.

## Thoughts and facts

Your thoughts shape your daily life. When negative thoughts dominate your mind, they harm your identity and distort your view of life. That's why the Bible stresses keeping your heart with all diligence: it raises the issues of life. When your mental state is bad, other parts of your life also feel like they are falling apart, even if they aren't. The happiness and positive outlook you need to have in life all start with being in a good mental state.

Overcoming negative thoughts isn't easy, especially when they persistently flood your mind. To stop negative thoughts, you must understand that the presence of a thought doesn't equate to it being true. Thoughts and facts are very different. Just because you think something doesn't make it true.

There's a huge difference between feelings due to something that happened and those from what people say about you. You don't choose what you go through or the storms in your life. But you can choose how to react to people's opinions. It's easy to criticise yourself for something you went through. But you don't want others' thoughts to define those criticisms. If you do, you'll carry a heavier burden. It will be your thoughts and others' opinions of you.

The enemy's biggest goal is to make you believe your past defines you. He wants you to dwell on what you went through and never find freedom from it. He wants you to believe that people's opinions matter more than what God sees and says about you. If you define yourself by others' opinions, your life will be unstable. People's opinions about you will always change. You need to place your identity on something stable. Otherwise, you'll spend your life searching for yourself and never find you. Past experiences can cast a shadow over who you truly are but cannot erase your identity. The struggles to understand who you are don't take away the fact that you have an identity. Your identity still exists. It's just hard to see it, given all you've been through.

**How to overcome negative thoughts**

When you have a negative thought, the first thing you may want to do is push that negative thought away. It's natural to want to distract yourself from them. But the truth is, the more you try to suppress those thoughts, the more powerful they become. The key to overcoming negative thoughts is to face them instead of sweeping them away. When you face them, they often lose their power and become easier to manage.

The Bible says to "bring every thought into captivity and make it obedient to Christ." This means rejecting every negative thought that contradicts what God says about you. Don't just distract yourself from them. Remember, the goal isn't just to stop your thoughts. It's to replace them with what's true. Sweeping thoughts away means they will always return. That's why holding the thought and training your mind to believe the facts about you is powerful.

For example, a negative thought could be telling you that you will forever be alone and that no one cares about you. That isn't true. God will never leave or forsake you. So, when you feel like you will be alone forever, remind yourself, "God will never leave me or forsake me." Doing this repeatedly trains your mind. It teaches you that not every thought is true. Most importantly, it replaces the lie with the facts about your life.

The enemy will take advantage of the negative life-changing situations. He will also attempt to use your experiences to form and mould your identity to what he wants you to be. If you know who you are, you can resist him; hence, why he tries to keep you in the dark, so he can stay in charge. He tries to trap you in darkness by targeting your mind. As long as the enemy has power over your mind, he can have power over your life. Remember, the past may have shaped you to be who you are right now, but it can never fully define your life unless you let it.

### The woman with the issue of blood

In the Bible, there's a lady who was suffering from a blood issue for 12 years. The Bible says that she tried everything, going to doctors and even spending her last penny. Nothing she tried stopped the issue of blood that she had.

Unfortunately, the Bible doesn't state her name. Since she had this problem for 12 years, her community only knew her as nothing but the lady with the issue of blood. One can only imagine the negative comments that circled the community about her. One day, Jesus was going down to her town. She was finally going to come into contact with the one who can heal her from this 12-year-long issue. The moment finally came. After seeing Him, the woman went behind Jesus to touch His garment. She had gotten to a point of desperation. She believed a touch of his garment would cure her issue. How she approached Jesus says a lot. It reveals how she saw herself and how he had been in her community. Her going behind Jesus puts more stress on the fact that she had many insecurities. She had been isolated for so long that hiding became second nature to her. Even when she was in the presence of God, she hid; little did she know that with Jesus, it's different.

She spent many years in shame and hearing others negative opinions. But, at the sight of Jesus, everything changed for her. Once Jesus noticed she had touched his clothes, He asked the crowd who it was that had touched His garment. I still believe that He did this intentionally so that she could be seen for the first time. In the end, what Jesus did for this woman was make sure she got more than what she originally came to receive. He healed her body and her brokenness. He gave her an identity worth keeping. Jesus claimed her by calling her daughter and made her feel loved and seen. How the community saw her may not have changed. They may still see her as a woman with an issue of blood. But what they thought didn't matter. The day she met Jesus, everything about her changed. She understood that what Jesus said about her was all that mattered. Jesus affirming her and telling her that she was his daughter made all the difference. Jesus built her confidence and gave her a solid foundation to walk on.

**Healing from things which leave you empty**

Becoming like the woman with the issue of blood is easy. The challenge lies in unlearning and becoming who she changed into when she met Jesus. It takes courage to admit that your efforts to heal did nothing but leave you empty.

Like the woman, there are some issues you will have in life that no one but Jesus can cure. You may know that only Jesus can help you. But, it's only when you become desperate and run out of choice that's when many run to what they already knew was the cure.

Most of the time, the things you may do end up leaving you less fulfilled than when you started. The woman with the issue of blood knew that Jesus could heal her because she had faith in him. She only understood that Jesus was the only cure once everything she tried had failed her. The lady with the issue of blood had a blood problem. In trying to heal herself, she became poor. Your efforts to heal can create new problems on top of the ones you are currently trying to deal with.

**Your true identity**

Your sense of self comes from a mix of the things you've been through and what others think of you. These two things shape how you see yourself. Things like betrayal, heartbreak and emotional abuse create negative changes in your life. Endless negative experiences make it easy to see your life negatively and believe others' opinions about it. For example, a person who faces constant abuse will have feelings of worthlessness. So, if someone labels them as unworthy, there is a tendency to believe it easily. The negative opinion confirms the feelings of unworthiness they already have towards themselves. Making it easier for them to believe that it's true. As time goes by, you start to focus on the bad stuff people say about you and overlook the good stuff. That's when negative thoughts and opinions start to weigh heavier than positive ones.

What people say about you versus what Christ says about you are two different things. Here's the thing: people's opinions about you will always change depending on what you do or don't do. The thing you need to know about people is that what they think or say about you will always change depending on what you do or don't do. Today, you might do something that makes people look at you in a good light. Then, the week after, you could do something that makes people look down on you. With Jesus, it's not like that. Whatever you do will never change how He sees you.

People's opinions can blur your vision, hiding the real truth. If you focus too much on what others think, you'll start to doubt what God says is true. Don't forget your value comes from God's words, not what others say. To fully know who you truly are, you need to look at the facts about you. That's why identity isn't just about knowing who you are but knowing who you are from the right source. Once you learn the facts, believe them and live by them. People's opinions will never matter to you, and if they ever do, you will know they don't change the facts about you. When you get to know God, you will get to know you.

Once you find your core identity, there will be times when you may not reflect it. The core identity is still there. It just isn't reflected in your current season. There's a time and season for everything. Seasons change but your identity doesn't change with them. On your healing journey, you'll feel worthless at times. You'll be confused about who you are and who you're becoming. Find comfort in knowing that seasons change as a reminder that nothing lasts forever. Life's dark seasons will eventually give away to the bright ones. The good times might become bad. But this cycle of change gives hope that no matter what season you are in, it doesn't last forever.

**Your identity is hidden in Christ.**

The woman with the issue of blood was already the daughter of Jesus, but she didn't know it. That's why when she gets healed, he tells her, 'Be of good cheer, daughter. Your faith has made you well.' Jesus didn't want to only heal her from the disease she had been struggling with for all these years. He was so intentional about her that he made sure she was healed and that she left knowing she was His daughter. Before, she only saw herself through the lens of her pain and people's opinions. By reaffirming her, Jesus let her know that despite all that, she still had value. Her situation didn't change who she was or how Jesus saw her. Being made in the image of God means that you will only get to know yourself when you get to know him first. So when identity is the struggle, God is the solution. God made you one of a kind, knowing you better than you know yourself. Whenever self-doubt sneaks up, remember that your creator knows the real you. Life experiences can crush you. But in the end, God uses what should have crushed you to build you instead. Your past and the world's views may distort your identity. But you can know your true self by knowing God. This comes through praying to Him daily and asking Him to help you, and if you don't know what to ask for, then let Him know that. Then He will show you what you need.

**Pauline's story**

I was drained by the fact that I was depressed. I became tired of being stuck in one place, but I didn't know God was able to change me and save me from my trauma. It was hard for me to believe that I could be better than the person who the past had made me to be. I was in a dark hole for so many years. It convinced me I would never be better than the girl hidden in there.

The hole was my comfort zone; I had accepted who I was to the point where I was not eager to find out who I could have been. As years went by, I started to feel unsettled with the fact that I hadn't been happy for a long time. I started to feel desperate because I didn't want to feel the way I had been feeling. I was so mentally far away that each day, it weighed me down. Despite the battle being in my mind, it started feeling more physical; I didn't want to do anything. I was happy just sitting around, sleeping and scrolling on my phone. Well, I had convinced myself that my happiness was in these things. I'd be honest: I wasn't that close to Jesus. I believed He could do something with my life, but I wasn't sure if He could change it completely. That's how hopeless my situation looked in my eyes. After years of battling, I decided to give up. I gave up fighting something I couldn't win. Instead, I let God into those broken parts of me. Not one part of my life, by the way. My whole life. I had come to the conclusion that if I wanted true transformation, I needed to give my life back to the one who gave it to me.

One day, I was spending time with God by reading my Bible when I suddenly felt this overwhelming presence. I had never felt so loved in my life, and I don't think I ever will. He used those around me to show that I was loved. Most importantly, He used his word to show His love. I finally saw that my lonely journey wasn't so lonely. He was walking with me all along; I just ignored Him. I've also come to realise that it's not that I didn't have an identity. Rather, my identity was hidden. It was hidden behind all the pain, abuse, betrayal and all the rejection. That's why, when the mess was removed, I could for once start seeing myself for who I truly was. That's the beauty of Jesus. He shows you things that were already there, but you were blind to. You would only have known them if He had shown you. I thought my healing journey would come in the craziest way possible. I didn't think healing would be like this. I almost gave up, thinking it had to be as intense as what I went through. I thought my healing had to equate to my trauma. But then I found out healing can be pretty straightforward when God's the healer.

My healing journey was difficult. It was lonely, it was crushing, and a lot of unlearning was done. I didn't think I'd ever see life after trauma, but I'm living in the abundance of it. God's changed everything about me. I don't look like what I've been through. I'm whole, and I've found my true identity, which doesn't look like the one trauma gave me.

He gave me peace, which doesn't make sense, and shaped parts of me that I didn't even realise were broken. God knows your needs better than you do. He knows you more than you know yourselves. So, when He starts to transform and mould you, trust Him.

**Advice**

Believing people's opinions is easier if what they say is how you already see yourself. Many bad experiences in childhood can harm your self-image. Others' negative ideas and poor treatment can make you have low self-esteem. The good part is the thing you have been through or are going through may break you. But God will make you again. He will mend all the broken little pieces and make you a whole piece. He will restore your identity.

Finding your identity in Christ doesn't mean people will see you as Jesus does. They may still have the same image of you and the same opinions about you, but that doesn't matter. This is all about you knowing who you are, not trying to prove to people that you are something different. It's not your business to prove that God has changed you. Let the change speak for itself. It's hard to believe God can do it for you when the trauma has lasted a long time. But with Jesus, there's nothing He can't do. What looks impossible in your eyes is more than possible with Jesus.

# Worth

Your self-image is shaped by your experiences, others' opinions and your achievements. Self-worth comes from reassuring yourself with what you know. Meaning your worth can be easily swayed. Your worth needs to have a solid standing. What I mean by that is that the worth needs to be set on a solid foundation that never changes.

Worth is more than self-perception. If that wasn't the case, when you break the boundaries you set, you would feel less worthy. There would always be this neediness to do something to be more worthy when worth should be something that you have without doing anything.

Viewing yourself how God sees you changes your outlook on yourself. It means that you still see your value even when you mess up. Knowing your worth comes from God's opinion of you will keep you steady no matter what the world says about you. Imagine being loved and accepted no matter what. Not because of what you've done or what you have, but just because you're precious.

When you start experiencing the lows of life, it's easy in these moments to think less of yourself. Getting caught up in negative self-talk is easy when things aren't going your way. But remembering that your identity is rooted in God's love can help silence those voices. You start to see that your value doesn't come from what you do or don't do. Instead, it comes from the unchanging love of the one who created you.

Emotional maturity is knowing you can't believe your thoughts when you are feeling low. For example, if your thoughts tell you that you are worthless, you know these aren't based on reality. How God sees you will never change. His truth about you and your life stays the same even when life experiences go against it. When doubts arise, remember that you are worthy no matter your circumstances. Nothing can change how God sees you. So, nothing should change how you see yourself. Getting to the point of seeing yourself the way God sees you means that people's opinions won't matter. It doesn't mean that you won't be put down by opinions, but rather that it doesn't remove the value you as a person hold.

God is the same yesterday, today and forever. If God doesn't change, then the way He sees you won't change either. When you see yourself how God sees you, you have power because your worth isn't based on an experience. But it's based on what the true living God says about you. People can't get to you and try to shame you about your past. They can't bring you down by pointing at the trauma you faced. They can't trigger you by reminding you of the words the person you loved so much said to you. Your worth doesn't lie in the things you've been through. Your worth doesn't lie in the trauma anymore. You know you are worthy simply because God says that you are, and God sees that you are. Your past doesn't define you anymore, meaning that the way it made you see yourself doesn't define you either.

### Worth in relationships

I got into my first relationship at 17. After the sexual abuse had stopped, I found myself yearning for love. I craved male affection to compensate for the love I didn't receive. I was eager for that love. So, I tolerated many things in my relationship that I now wouldn't accept.

Receiving love for me came at a cost, as I always found myself acting blind to the red flags. I sacrificed my well-being because I was willing to accept any love that was thrown at me, even if that love was mixed with some thorns. At the end of the day, all I needed was someone to show me they cared.

The relationship was clearly damaging to both of us, but the thought of not being in it left me empty. I did everything that I could to make sure that we stayed together. I began to glamorise my ex-boyfriend's potential. I couldn't stay with him for who he was, so I started seeing him as who I wished he could have been, and that kept the relationship surviving for long enough. After a while, I became so attached to the point that I couldn't let go. The longer I stayed, the more I became unhealthily attached. On several occasions, I wanted to end the relationship, but I feared being alone. I never had the courage to leave.

I was convinced my ex-boyfriend was the only toxic one in our relationship. But I played a really big part in its failure. I was tired of being tired, so day and night, I prayed to God to make the relationship walk away from me. What God did for me instead was He made me see my worth. The toxic relationship was being fed with the fact that I didn't know my value. I'll admit that I did jump in and out of the relationship, but once I understood how God sees me, I never went back.

Everything in life is either a blessing or a lesson. For me, this relationship taught me a lesson I will carry with me for years to come. It taught me who I choose to date is greatly influenced by how I perceive myself. Suppose you don't value yourself the way you need to. In that case, you will form relationships with people who undervalue you. Looking back at your partners in the past, you find you only went for them because you didn't know yourself. You may have gotten into relationships to get validation and fill the void left by your lack of self-love. That's where the problem is. Seeking validation from others only gives you reasons to undervalue yourself. When they don't approve of you, you are left trying to show them why you are worthy. That is something you shouldn't have to do.

**You are valuable. You just need to know it.**

One day, she heard Jesus was going to be in her town. She went to visit the town where there was a multitude of people surrounding Jesus. There were many people, but she managed to get close enough to him. She didn't know that the encounter she would have with Jesus would change her life forever. This is the moment she went behind Jesus and touched His garment. Before she knew it, she had found healing from her 12-year-long disease. After touching Him, Jesus went to ask the crowd who touched him because he felt it. He called her out so as not to shame or embarrass her. He wanted to show her that even in a crowd, her existence mattered to Him. Even in a huge crowd, He was still intentional about her life. Back to the story, this lady said it was her who had touched His garment. What Jesus does after is so warm and reassuring. Jesus calls her daughter. He tells her to be of 'good comfort' and to 'go in peace.

The lady's intention was to touch Jesus to receive physical healing. But Jesus gave her more than that because He knew that she had a physical issue, but she also had an identity issue. He reaffirmed that, despite what people said, she was still worthy of being called His daughter. He showed her that she was special to him and that he was intentional about her life. At this moment, she knew that if Jesus knew her issue in a crowd of 1000s, it meant He saw when she felt alone and insecure and wished it would go away. He saw her discouraged and hopeless days.

I say all this to say that God sees you the same despite what you have been or will ever go through. Some things you go through may have isolated you, made you feel ashamed and led you to hide away. But even with all that, God still considers you valuable and deserving to be seen. He loves you, and He cherishes you. Like the woman with the issue of blood, she was insecure. She was used to hiding due to what her village said about her.

God still deemed her valuable, and nothing can ever change that. The difference between you now and who you are going to become is knowing your value. The woman with the issue of blood was valuable all along, but she didn't know that. You are still valuable even in that dark pit you are isolated in. You just can't comprehend it yet. Knowing it is what will make a difference in your life. Learning how Jesus sees you will teach you how to love yourself.

**People and you**

Sometimes, the way you treat yourself indicates and gives people a hint of how they should treat you. That's why you see the same person treating different people differently.

Other times, some people will treat you how they treat themselves. So, their actions toward you are a projection of how they see themselves. This could be positive or negative, where they project their insecurities onto you. The harsh reality of life is that people around you may not treat you the way you deserve to be treated.

You do have the power to walk away and free yourself from their control. Insecurities will try to hold you back. They can get the better of you and make you cling to what's already expired. Afraid to let go, you stay in places you don't belong anymore. You find yourself stuck in spaces, relationships and friendships that are no longer working out. To know your worth is to know you are valuable and leave when something tries to prove otherwise. Understand that how people treat you doesn't reflect how worthy you are. How people treat you doesn't have an impact on your value. Their lack of love towards you doesn't equate to no value.

**Your insecurities**

One insecurity can diminish and dismiss all the good qualities that you have. Naaman was a man in the bible who was a leaper. The bible mentions Naaman's most remarkable qualities. It mentions that he was highly respected. It even goes to say that the Lord had given victory to the Syrian forces because of him. That's how much of a great guy Naaman was. Towards the end of that verse, it says that 'he was a great soldier, "BUT" he suffered from a dreaded skin disease.' Naaman was a fantastic man. All his good qualities were so impressive that they dismissed the fact that he had a skin disease. Yet, using the word "but" makes you forget Naaman's good qualities. All of a sudden, your attention shifts to the insecurities he had.

Just like Naaman, you may have all these great characteristics and good things about you. And the good things about you far outweigh the one thing you have that's not great. You focus more on your flaws instead of embracing all the great things about you. Insecurities make you forget your good traits and fixate on small flaws. God sees you differently than you see yourself. He also sees you differently than the negative views others have of you. He sees a different version of the insecure image you have of yourself. It's about time you started seeing yourself as the person God sees you as.

**Pauline's story**

I still lived with my father a few years after the abuse. He said a lot of abusive words towards me that I couldn't even imagine saying to my worst enemy. Certain phrases said, especially being at such a young age, cut deep. It almost felt like someone was piercing my heart with each degrading comment I received.

Sometimes, the pain of the words felt physical. It left me in a deep sadness, which kept me crying the whole night, rethinking my whole existence. It startled me that my father could be abusing me and at the same time, be saying all of these things.

I remember pointing a finger at myself and reaffirming that I'm cheap. As a child, it was easy to believe everything he said. At the end of the day, he was supposed to want the best for me, so there was no doubt that what he was saying was true. The longer I sat on the thoughts, the more they sank in. Only when I became much older did I learn that I was far from what he said to me. I stopped reaffirming myself with the words my earthly father said. I focused on reaffirming myself using the words my heavenly father says about me. I shifted my focus and started looking at myself through the lens of my heavenly father. If I continued believing what my father said to me, I would still be stuck in the same hole he dug for me.

My father's imperfections became clear to me, so I didn't need to believe what he said about me. Why would a flawed person's opinion about me matter when I can believe what my perfect heavenly father says about me?

My father's words were a mere projection. It's a shame I had to bear the consequences of them. Learning that not every opinion should be taken was a game-changer for me.

For some time, the things my father was saying to me made me feel like I was a problem. Or even worse, that I was doing things that made him act the way he did towards me. My life changed when I removed my guilt. I finally understood how my father treated me was a mere projection of my father's internal feelings. It had nothing to do with who I was. For once, I fully understood that it wasn't a me issue but a him problem. Finding my value wasn't an overnight journey. Learning my value meant I understood that I may have been through some stuff, but that doesn't take away from who I am. I may have been through abuse and struggled to heal from it, but even with all of that, my value is still the same. There's nothing I had gone through that changed that.

It was easy to hear that I was valuable, but the real challenge was whether I believed it myself. I had learned how God saw me, but now I had to see myself the way He saw me. The Bible reminded me that "my life is hidden in Christ." That meant everything. It meant that by knowing God, I would know myself. If my life is hid in Christ, it means this: When I know him, I will start to see myself how He sees me. Not as my trauma had shaped me to see myself, but as the creator of this universe sees me. That was the game changer for me. As I prayed, read the Bible, and did daily affirmations, the more I got closer to God, the more I knew who I was.

**They will never be able to steal your value.**

Going through abuse can cause you to question your own value. How they treated you doesn't help; it makes you doubt yourself even more. If you had known how precious you are, you would not tolerate some behaviours and treatments from others. An unloving childhood led you to believe you are worthless and unlovable. Once you unlearn, confront these false narratives. Replace them with the truth. You will know your pure existence alone makes you worthy.

## Advice

Just in case nobody has told you yet. They may have stolen something from you, but one thing they can never steal from you is your value. No one will ever be able to steal your value. Sometimes, you may feel like your worth is fluctuating, and it's normal to feel like that. Don't let that feeling confuse you with what is true. Your worth doesn't change depending on your actions or how people treat you. Sometimes, it may feel like it, but how people treat you doesn't reflect your value.

There's nothing in this life that can happen to you that can change your value. You are still precious despite your experiences. You are still worthy despite what others say about you or how they treat you. Your value will never change because how God sees you will never change. As you embark on this path, you will begin to realise that the person you thought you were is not the person God created you to be. The weight of trauma will slowly lift, and you will start to see yourself through God's eyes rather than the distorted lens of your past.

# Doubtless doubts

Lewis Pugh said something I really love: "Doubt your doubts before you doubt yourself." I think about this a lot because of how true it is. Plus, it's what people who struggle with doubts wish they could do. The first thing you need to know about doubtful thoughts is that they don't come out of nowhere. You don't just wake up one day and start doubting. It grows, gets big, and then starts to affect your daily life. Your past plays a big part in who you are. Doubt is one of those things you don't realise is brought up by your experiences and how people made you feel.

The funny thing about doubtful thoughts is that they will always concern something you really want for yourself. For example, I grew up in a village in Kenya with little to nothing but enough to keep us going daily. Being in the village, I didn't have anything to compare that life to, so it looked like we were living in abundance. When I came to London, I finally had something to compare my village life to.

The change from village to city life was so drastic it was almost hard to comprehend. I was living in a village one day, then literally a month later, I was in this big city with so many buildings that I never even thought would exist. A few years after settling into London life, I realised my family's wealth was low compared to that of Londoners. Everything looked amazing back in the village because that's all I could see. When I saw another better way of living, I became very eager to succeed. I didn't only want to help my immediate family, but I wanted it to go beyond and help other families who were struggling to make ends meet. Success was something I woke up and slept thinking about. I knew my success would be life-changing. It would create opportunities to help those who couldn't help themselves. I was willing to work hard to succeed.

My doubtful thoughts started getting the better of me when I compared my goals to my life situation. I was a young, broken child with zero motivation to do anything, let alone work hard. I had the passion, but I almost felt chained and restricted.

Every idea stayed an idea because everything I wanted for my future seemed impossible, so I didn't bother trying. Having overcome doubtful thoughts, I now know they don't just affect the present. If not dealt with, they go further into affecting your future and tarnishing your goals.

Doubtful thoughts are more damaging when the doubted idea is something you really want for yourself. That could be, in a small sense, like doubting your crush will genuinely like you. Or in a bigger sense, like about your aspirations and the things you want to achieve. If the area you doubted wasn't something you care about, the thoughts wouldn't be so destructive. All it takes is a single consistent thought to completely change your mind and actions towards something. The goal is to make your mind and actions team up to fight against doubt so the battle when it comes to doubt can be won. You must overcome doubt because your growth depends on your state of mind!

**Doubt as a defence mechanism**

Doubt can be a defence mechanism that can protect you when things don't go how you expected them to. In that case, it means that doubt can be used as a shield. After a lifetime of bad things happening all the time, you become sceptical of good things. To protect yourself from any pain that will come from the good things that happen, you don't put too much hope that it will last anyway. When that good thing eventually goes wrong, you won't be shocked. Your doubt has shielded you from any hurt it would have caused. It's defensive, and at least by doubting, you can say you saw it coming when really you didn't. You just always believe every good thing will turn bad and hurt you again. There's nothing wrong with being cautious and having foresight, but using doubt as a defence for everything isn't wise. It's not the best to always assume things will go wrong. Have faith that things will work out. You lose nothing by hoping for the good. God wants the best for you, and he says he knows his plans for you. Plans to prosper you and give you an expected end. Not to say you won't face challenges on your journey to success, but to say that God doesn't want evil in your life. He wants to see you happy and wants you to be the head and not the tail. Putting yourself on more optimistic ground is scary. It's worse if you

# 81

had an unpredictable childhood. Removing this shield of doubt teaches you that not all good things will go bad. If things don't go as you expected, removing this shield forces you to deal with unexpected outcomes. It helps you cope with the ups and downs.

Have faith that things will go well, so when they don't, you know it is not due to a lack of belief. It is just that things did not go well.

**Doubt and the good things**

Once you place a ripe fruit next to a rotten one, it rots quicker than if it were left by itself. When doubt infiltrates the good things in your life, this is what unfolds. Good things may end, but doubt makes them end sooner.

A tough childhood can lead to a negative view of life. The good things did happen, but the bad things outweighed them. In the end, you feel a constant sense of negativity, and it just seems like everything in your life sucks. With time, this wears away your hope and leaves you feeling like having a good life is impossible and out of reach.

Good things will happen. Your role is to allow them to flourish while they last instead of shortening their lifespan. This doesn't mean that every good thing that happens will be a great fairy tale. It also doesn't mean that every good thing that happens will be a disaster. It's a reminder to do your best in each season of your life and embrace everything in life. Focus on the bright side of life. That way, you can fully enjoy the good times. Don't let the bad sides overshadow and take away your joy.

**Doubt puts an end to opportunities**

Doubt will always belittle your potential because it puts an end to something before it fully grows. Ending something before it happens means you can't show up as intended. You have already added fear and doubt that it will go nowhere. The fear makes you shrink, meaning you fail to fulfil whatever you were supposed to be doing to its fullest potential. You miss out on the benefits it could give. Relationships are a good example of this. Someone who never received love while growing up might downplay a romantic relationship due to their troubled childhood. They might feel unworthy and unloveable due to their experiences. They may even mentally put an end to the relationship by doubting the other party's affection and thinking they will be hurt or the relationship won't last. Considering the exit door without reason means they will never be who they are supposed to be in the relationship. Of many reasons, doubt could be why some relationships fail.

Showing up with maximum efficiency in your life makes a huge difference. Sometimes, you may create delusions for yourself. You may see things as fantasy rather than what they are. Then, you pursue that idea, which doesn't exist. Be the best you can be in every moment, and don't feed on the delusions created in your mind. When you find yourself feeding on your delusions, stop and reflect. Ask yourself if the thought I'm having is a result of something that happened or if it is a result of my existing insecurities. Sometimes, what you have been through can be the catalyst for your doubtful thoughts.

### Gut feeling and doubt

Always trust your gut feelings while acknowledging they can be wrong sometimes. You may confuse your gut feelings with your doubtful thoughts. Having a gut feeling about something, not realising that sometimes doubts can be disguised as gut feelings. When gut feelings and doubt are mixed, it's hard to separate the two and know which is which. This is where guidance from God will help you. God knows everything. So, you can rest assured that He knows your daily thoughts. If you are doubtful and feel like you are having a gut feeling, don't dismiss it. Instead, seek confirmation from God and ask if it is a true gut feeling or just a disguised, doubtful thought. Then, when you get discernment from God, you can tell the difference between them.

The only way I was able to tell the difference between my gut feelings and doubtful thoughts was that my gut feelings came out of nowhere, but my doubts could be traced. Intuition often pops up when you least expect it, while your doubtful thoughts usually come from clear sources. They were always linked to something I had experienced or something I was told. When it came to gut feelings, I always had a physical sign in my body, like a feeling in the pit of my stomach. I noticed that my gut feelings were unfiltered responses, but doubtful thoughts had a build-up of things which led to them.

**Doubt and God's power**

One Friday evening, after finishing all the tasks for the day, I went up to my room and was ready to wind down and relax. I had a routine of showering, eating, and then sitting down before scrolling on my social media. This time, it was different. I decided to sit and scroll through my social media for a bit before showering.

Now, it was time for my shower, and I decided to look at myself in the mirror while getting ready to go. As I looked into the mirror, several doubtful thoughts started shooting at me.

*'I doubt you are ever going to find peace.'*

*'I doubt you are ever going to be successful enough to help your family.'*

*'I doubt what people say about you is true, and I bet they are lying.'*

*'I doubt you are ever going to do anything good.'*

This was unusual. I had doubted more before. But, I had never had so many doubts cloud my brain all at once. As the thoughts spiralled through my mind, I stood there devastated, crying my heart out, wishing I could control them. I didn't want to be negative all the time. I wanted to break free from my self-doubt and embrace a more positive outlook on life. A short while later, I suddenly felt a calm peace. I thought nothing of it though. Previously, when I'd have extreme emotions, I'd be calm a little later, so the sudden calmness was nothing new to me. Now, I had come out of my shower, gotten myself ready, and finally started having dinner. One of my other routines was watching a YouTube video every time I had something to eat. I remember eagerly searching for a fun YouTube video. But I had somehow watched all the popping videos released that week. I found nothing. Then I scrolled down a little and stumbled on a YouTube video titled 'Wrestling Doubts.' I was caught by surprise because my doubtful thoughts had attacked me before this. Immediately I became eager to know the content and message of the video.

As the lady was speaking, I felt more relieved as she went on because it was as though she was speaking to me directly.

Everything mentioned in the video had my name on it, and this left me emotional. As the video progressed and neared the end, she began to speak about doubt and God's power. She mentioned that doubtful thoughts doubt God's power. I didn't understand this right away. But, as the day passed, it resonated with my spirit. I later realised that the devil had used my past to plant doubts in my mind, which meant I was questioning God's power over my life without realising it. They were causing me to question what God could do for me. Without noticing it, I was making it look like the devil has so much power over my life when he doesn't. The enemy can only do as much as God allows, and he, indeed, doesn't have much power anyway. The enemy's strategy works best when you are at your weakest; he isn't able to get you when you are at your strongest. That's why he waits for your most vulnerable moments to attack your life.

He will use your past to make you doubt God's power. Thinking about the doubtful thoughts you have had, you realise that they are all things that God can do. He can do more than you can imagine. But the enemy doesn't want you to believe that. When you doubt, you question God's power in your lives.

**Advice**

The enemy is already afraid of you and your potential, so the most he can do is make sure he makes you doubt. He focuses on making you doubt the areas of your life where there's evidence of why you should doubt. The enemy cannot stop you, so he tries to delay you. He wants to keep you from fulfilling your purpose. He does this by sowing doubt, trapping you in a cycle. But God makes the possible out of impossible situations.

God's thoughts toward you are thoughts of peace, not of evil. He wants to give you an expected end. This is what God says and promises about you and your life. He is more powerful than the thoughts you are having. Remember, any thought you have which doesn't align with this isn't from God. The devil's thoughts are deceiving. They aim to distract you from what can help you. They are there to keep you focused on the things you can't control rather than the one who controls everything. At the end of the day, all that matters is God's promises for you because you are His. God wants to give you hope. The devil intends evil. If you focus on the devil's power, it will be harder to see God's power in your life.

# Environments

Living in an environment that harms you can lead to constant defeat and frustration. The situation is even more frustrating when you are unable to leave. It's common to think that moving to a different location will ease your pain. But a change in environment is only able to take all the pain away if it's the root cause of your pain.

When that's not the case, changing environments may not end the pain. But it will provide you with a calm and safe place to reflect. In the Bible, a girl named Tamar, unfortunately, suffered the consequences of her brother's lust. She had two brothers named Absolom and Ammon.

The perpetrator, Ammon, who was her half-brother, had become full of lust towards Tamar. He and his friend worked on a plot to help Ammon to be in a space with just him and her. It's then they decided that Ammon should play sick and demand for Tamar to cook for him. He pretended he couldn't feed himself due to the 'extreme sickness.' It happened that Tamar was told to cook for him. After she had finished, he demanded that she come into the room and feed him. Tamar followed the instructions. She went into his bedroom, not imagining anything as bad as this would happen to her. It's this moment her disgusting brother preyed on her and stole her innocence. Tamar felt deep shame. She tore her dress and covered herself with ashes to show that she had been violated and was mourning. The sexual violence stole her identity, and poor Tamar was never the same again. After this traumatic moment, she went to live with her other brother Absolom in his house. Though Tamar was no longer in the place where she was abused, she still felt desolate and empty. Tamar's innocence was stolen, and that affected her both physically and emotionally.

Her new environment helped keep her away from the constant reminders of what her brother did to her, but it couldn't change how his actions affected her. For her to find freedom past the desolate feeling she had, she needed to heal from the trauma itself. I share this story to say that the reason you are hurting isn't because of the place you were in but because of what happened in that environment. Healing from painful experiences means finding the root of your desolation and loneliness. Sometimes, that can mean leaving the environment where you got bruised.

**The environment is just a catalyst for your pain.**

It's easier to point fingers at an environment as the reason for your pain, especially if you're unsure about why you're feeling the way you are. Take a bedroom as an example because it is a comfort zone for many. It's a place where most individuals have privacy and can do whatever they want. For some, after a long day of being busy at work or school, the bedroom is where they get to tap back into their reality. The bedroom then becomes a place where they experience their negative emotions. It's where they finally wind down and feel what was hidden by their busy schedule. Outside the bedroom, they are happy, but when in it, their mood shifts. They blame the environment for their changing emotions. But the root of their emotions lies within. Sometimes, you can only benefit from a new environment after you overcome your mental struggles. At the end of the day, the battle is within, so no matter where you go, you can't escape your inner conflicts. With that being said, an immediate change of location may be necessary.

Not everyone will have the strength to stay in the place where they got hurt while working to fight inner battles. Challenges will always exist. But, some places ease the struggle. They make it easier to win the battle in the mind.

**Pauline's story**

Since the abuser was my father, it meant that I had to live with him even after the abuse had stopped. While living with him, I constantly raged and felt fiery anger towards him. His presence in itself sent me into an unexplainable spiral of emotions. It didn’t matter that the abuse had stopped. Seeing him often, or even interacting with him, still brought back the same feelings I had during the abuse. There was a feeling of unsafety as if the abuse was happening again. I knew my journey to overcome this trauma would be hard, especially since every time I saw him, I was taken back to the place I’d been trying to escape. It annoyed me more because I found myself feeling angry without really meaning to. He didn’t have to do anything for the anger to rise up. Once I was able to change environments, I noticed that my pain hadn't gone away, but at the same time, I felt more at peace. For once in my life, I wasn't in the environment where the abuse took place, nor was I living with the person who did it. It's natural to feel a lot of emotions, like anger when you see someone who has hurt you before. Seeing them brings back vivid memories, and unhealed wounds start to hurt again.

That anger and resentment won't cool until you escape the abuser. To find peace, you need to step away from the situation and give yourself some space away from the person who caused you harm. The distance allows your feelings of anger and resentment to settle. Changing environments may not make the anger go away. But moving away stops it from getting worse. It stops the growth of your already existing anger.

**Advice for those staying in unhealthy environments**

Staying in a toxic environment that you have no choice but to stay in is draining. It's good to know how to navigate living in that environment before getting the opportunity to move away. Firstly, I will say accept the people you are staying with for who they are and don't live with a fantasied image of them.

Don't imagine who they could be or how they could behave. Judge their actions based on reality, not through the imagined versions of them. Taking them as they are means you are less disappointed when they act a certain way. It will still hurt your feelings. But their actions won't shock you. You see them who they are, not who you hope they could be, making you less surprised when they do something they promised they wouldn't.

**Toxic environments and growth**

Objects in a place where something traumatic occurred can revive memories. Being in those environments can trigger you and remind you of past experiences. Even if those events are over, being in similar places might bring back feelings you felt at that time. It can be hard to grow when you are in a negative environment. You can slowly grow and overcome some mental struggles.

Just like a plant, you can only reach your full height in good soil. Growing n negative environments is almost impossible. You can slowly grow and overcome some mental struggles. But you can only gain so much from surviving in a toxic environment. It will reach a point where a change of environment is essential to get to the next level of who you need to become. You can work hard to move forward. But, sooner or later, the environment will make you stagnant.

Weirdly, staying or being in the same place where a difficult event can reveal the areas you struggle with. For example, staying in the same house with my father helped me realise I needed to forgive him for my own sanity. I wouldn't have seen the need to forgive him if it wasn't for the fact that we had to live together. Seeing him every day showed me how angry I was at him. Anger stopped me from moving forward. It was unpleasant being around myself, and that's something I couldn't escape. I had to heal so I could face myself. The first step was forgiveness. I had to forgive him for what he did. And I had to forgive myself for being my worst enemy when I needed it most.

**Pauline's story**

Overcoming triggers is daunting. It requires you to confront the things that make you anxious and fearful. I used to have this thing I called door anxiety. Doors being opened used to be my biggest trigger. I had no issue with doors being opened when I wasn't there. But, when I was in a room with an open door, I felt tense and scared, as if I was hiding from something. Immediately after someone entered the room, I would tell them to make sure they closed the door.

This trigger came from the abuse I had faced. The abuse happened whenever my bedroom door was opened. I feared that the door being open meant that I was in danger and my father was going to walk through the door. There wasn't much of a difference when the door was locked. The abuse would have happened either way. However, I felt slightly safe. I had this moment of protection, even if it was for a little while. Even after the abuse had stopped, I would still feel the urge to protect myself by closing the door.

To overcome my severe door anxiety, I needed to understand why I always wanted the door closed. I flicked through my childhood memories and remembered why the locked door made 11-year-old me so relieved. Then, the next step was to face that trigger, confronting the anxiety connected to opening the door. Normally, the open door brought heavy anxiety; however, once it was closed, I was relieved. When facing the trigger, there wasn't any of this. Now, I had to fully feel the emotions that came up as a result of that trigger. But this time, I kept reassuring myself. The abuse was over. My father would not walk through there again and hurt me. As much as it was hard, it's also what helped me overcome this anxiety.

### Changing environments to make others feel the pain of losing you

Leaving an environment that doesn't support your growth can be tough, but it shows great courage and strength. Making this choice is challenging but is an important step for moving forward. When you choose to step away from a toxic situation, you are not only escaping negativity but also taking charge of your life again. This new sense of control can greatly improve your mental and emotional health, helping you rediscover what matters most to you. By making this brave choice, you start a positive change that can lead to a more fulfilling and meaningful life.

Leaving to make others feel the pain of losing you will bring you right back to the place you just left because your intentions are trauma-driven. And when your intentions are trauma-driven, and you don't get the reaction you want, you stop doing it. You could be fed up already, but that's not why you leave. You are leaving to get a reaction from them. Trying to make your tormentors feel your pain will only hurt you again. Most of the time, they are unaffected by you leaving. They won't give you the reaction you want, leaving you frustrated and lonelier. This can all be avoided by having the right intention when moving out. You don't ever need to prove a point by leaving. Instead, let your intention be to leave so you can prioritise your well-being. That way, you will be more empowered and confident in your decision. Making decisions while angry or annoyed will not accurately reflect what you want to do. It is wise to make a choice when you are calm. Think carefully before making a choice. Taking the time to consider your options can help you avoid regret and challenges later on.

## Healing in places which broke you

You can't properly heal in the places where you got hurt. Memories and emotions tied to those places trigger past traumas. This makes it hard to move forward. It's like a house that is on fire. A burning house remains dangerous even after extinguishing the fire. Even though there is no fire, the smoke becomes the new harm. The house still remains broken from the fire. It won't be safe to live in a house even without the fire and smoke. It's only possible for someone to live in a house like this once it is rebuilt and meets a decent survivable standard.

Notice that the effects of the fire and smoke will be different. The fire would burn you and create immediate pain. However, smoke will harm your lungs and cause damage in the long term. This example applies to environments and their effect on you even after the traumatic event has ended. The fire here represents the thing that physically hurt you. The trauma may not be happening anymore. But that doesn't mean you will be okay just because it has ended. You will feel certain emotions and triggers. You can only reduce them by leaving the place that causes these heightened feelings.

The only possible way to heal in an environment that broke you is if that environment is built up first.

If you have no choice but to stay in these environments, there are many things you are forced to have under control for you to live there. Discover strategies to navigate the environment without putting yourself at risk. But it's better to face the aftermath of bad situations in safe spaces. Avoid places that heighten your negative emotions.

**Elizabeth's story**

You only feel free if you mentally and physically remove yourself from the situation. You have to physically get away from it and have to mentally detach yourself from the person and have no contact with them. You shouldn't allow them to manipulate you or gaslight you, and that's one thing that has stuck with me. Now, no one can do these things to me, not in a relationship or a workplace. I will not allow anyone to manipulate, lie to, or gaslight me. This has made me stronger. It's controversial. Some people say the journey made them better, stronger people. Others say it ruined their lives. It depends on the person, and it depends on how you handle it.

My biggest takeaway has been that you can either take your situation and cry about it for the rest of your life and suffer or use it to improve your life. Do you know what I mean? Like it's your choice to pick what you want. You have that say in your life, and it's whatever you want to do. At first, I felt like putting myself down, I felt sorry for myself, and I felt angry at myself. But, over time, I decided to let go of that hurt and pain and say, "You know what? It's not my fault. So, I can hold onto this or let it go. I can live my life knowing it happened, but it won't happen again.

# Forgiveness

Forgiving someone is one thing, but forgetting the pain their actions caused you is another. It sounds easy when it's being said, but one day, you will want to release the pain of what they did to you but find it a struggle because your mind still clings to those feelings and replays memories which remind you of how much they hurt you.

Remember, forgiveness doesn't mean erasing the memories of the past or downplaying your pain. It means acknowledging that your wounds still hurt and choosing not to let negative emotions eat you up. While letting go is the start of healing your past wounds, remember that forgiveness needs strength and courage. On the other side of forgiveness lies a happier life that doesn't look like what their actions caused.

**Pauline's story**

Forgiving the person who abused me was a struggle that lasted for so long. As a child, I was often lost in a sea of emotions, not knowing how to navigate the storm inside me. But one thing I was certain of was that I needed an apology. My father showed no remorse for his actions. So, I made it my mission to show him how his actions were affecting me. From ages 11 to 15, I occasionally wrote a letter to my father. Sometimes, the letters were filled with hate and anger. Other times, they expressed suicidal thoughts. On good days, I simply asked for an apology. I would then place the letter somewhere no one would look at except for him, and then I hurried off to school. It's weird enough to say that while I was at school, I didn't think of the letter at all. But, on my way home, I was curious to see his reply. To no surprise, each day when I came home, I found that he had ignored the letter, ripped it up, and thrown away the message I had written.

I was so tired and desperate for love that I didn't care if their apology was sincere. I just wanted an "apology". Turns out apologising was hard for them to do, and a suicidal letter wasn't enough to alert them to stop. After years of having my pain dismissed by the one causing it, I made the decision to let go. I recognised the burden of my trauma could have only been lifted off me by God. Letting go and letting God was, in fact, the easier part of this journey. But, my unforgiving heart always took me a step back each time.

**The difference between forgiveness and reconciliation**

Reconciliation is a two-sided thing where both parties choose to forgive each other and are willing to restore the relationship they previously had. Forgiveness and reconciliation are both difficult. Many people think that they can't truly forgive someone unless the relationship is mended. But, if that were true, certain situations would be hopeless, leaving no room for forgiveness. The reality is not all relationships can be repaired. There may be situations whereby reconciliation will cause more harm than good. Sometimes, reconciliation can do more harm than good, especially when the offender doesn't want to acknowledge their wrongdoing. So, trying to reconcile with someone like this will drain you and may knock you off your back.

Forgiveness isn't about fixing the relationship or seeking an apology from the person who wronged you. In fact, it doesn't even require the other person to acknowledge their mistakes or take responsibility for their actions. That's what makes forgiveness so hard. Remember that when you choose to forgive, you aren't doing it for the benefit of the person who hurt you but for your own sake. Forgiveness doesn't justify what they did. By forgiving, you are choosing to recognise their offence and how much it hurt you while refusing to let it consume you.

Forgiveness is a choice you will have to make to break free from negative emotions. By doing so, you will release yourself from the anger and resentment you carry towards that person and in the end, you will find inner peace. Holding onto the anger and bitterness is what you may do in an attempt to hurt them back, but that only harms you. Instead, try to let go and focus on healing. Unforgiveness harms your well-being by fostering emotions like anger and hatred. Forgiveness frees you from anger and hate and brings you peace and happiness. You choose forgiveness to be free of the pain they caused you. Not because what they did wasn't that bad.

Forgiveness isn't like childhood when you'd forgive and become best friends with the person who stole your pencil. It's different in adulthood. It's no longer someone taking your pencil or someone not wanting to play with you anymore. Now, it's the betrayal from the friend you never expected it from. It's your pain being thrown right back in your face. It's you having to heal from traumas caused by others. And you see, these things won't just hurt for a short time. The pain stays until you are ready to let it all go. In cases like these, you don't need the person who hurt you to come on the journey with you. Leave them where they left you because there's so much more to your life than the power their actions hold over you.

Forgiveness doesn't always equate to rekindling relationships. It's healthy to forgive and leave the person in the past. You don't need to go back to the people you are healing from. They weren't there when you were a broken piece, nor do they deserve to be there with the new version of you that's yet to come. It's worth noting that not all relationships are worth reconciling. You may be willing to build the relationship, but the other person isn't. Consider if that's the type of person you would want to rebuild a relationship with in the first place.

## How does unforgiveness affect you

Most of the time, these people may not deserve your forgiveness. I didn't feel that the person who hurt me deserved my forgiveness at all. The hate I had towards them was unbearable. I had so many reasons I had lined up as to why I couldn't forgive them. But even with all those reasons, none of them were worth the heavy weight of hateful pain I carried. The reasons were all justified, but they weren't good enough for me to suffer inside. I had to choose. Should I carry these 10,000 reasons and burn with anger? Or should I work on letting go and forgiving them?

One thing about not forgiving is that you are the one who suffers. The hate and anger you show them in hopes that they will feel your pain does nothing but hurt you instead. The hatred takes your peace away while their life continues like normal. So what was supposed to be hurting them is really and genuinely hurting you. It brings out this bitter character in you, which makes it hard for you to grow in other areas of your life. Now, you can imagine how unforgiveness shapes every other aspect of your life. This is why letting go of the 1,000 reasons to not forgive will be the best thing for you. It will let your heart feel the joy and peace God intended. While allowing you to find freedom in every other aspect of your life.

**They aren't remorseful**

Forgiving is hard. It gets harder if the person who hurt you shows no remorse for their behaviour. An apology can make it easier to forgive someone, but not everyone gets one. Often, you may wait for a long time in hopes that the person who hurt you will apologise for what they did. Most times though, this isn't the case. Not everyone who hurts you will even want to admit that they did hurt you in the first place. In cases like this, you will wait for eternity for an apology. One thing I know now that I wish someone had told me before is that not everyone who hurts you will be sorry about it. Some people will hurt you, and they won't even care. It's a hard pill to swallow. But knowing this makes the journey slightly easier. For once, you understand that healing from trauma isn't based on whether you get an apology. It's more about choosing yourself despite never being chosen. It means going on a journey through your darkness to see the light hidden by all your trauma. It looks easy when written on a page. But living in a dark space while trying to see the light is very exhausting. You will have emotions like anger and resentment. These will take you back to the place you have been trying to escape. My advice to you is that the journey to forgiveness isn't easy; otherwise, everyone would be doing it. What they did to you gives you every reason to resent and have hate towards them. I get you. The harder task is being honest with yourself and admitting that their actions hurt you and are still hurting you. But, for your own sake and well- being, you need to let it go. At the end of the day, you are the one suffering from their actions and the struggle of forgiving them. That's a hard decision you must make, but it will be the best decision you would have made for yourself. In terms of my story, I only started becoming happier once I'd forgiven my father. It was hard, don't get it twisted, but by forgiving him, I showed myself that I know how to choose me. The same goes for you. Forgiving them is a sign of self-love towards yourself.

**Emotions which grow from un-forgiveness**

You want the person who hurt you to feel your pain. So, you try to make them feel it by holding a grudge against them. If you forgive them, it would look like the person who hurt you is getting a shortcut and escaping what they did. Their actions caused you trauma and pain. So, you want to burden them with your unforgiveness to balance the harm they did. Holding a grudge won't hurt the person you resent. It will only hurt you more, even though that is not what you want. This whole idea creates a stronger hold on your life. You create a plan to destroy someone else. But it ends up attacking you instead of the person it is aimed towards. It attacks you by stirring up emotions like bitterness, when you see them living their life like nothing happened. You become angry at the fact that they don't acknowledge what they did hurt you. As bitterness lingers, it overwhelms you. It keeps you focused on the things that they did and makes you stuck in the past.

A gentle reminder that you have every reason to be mad and angry about what happened, but don't stay angry. It costs you your well-being to stay angry. All these emotions bring a lack of peace in your life.

**Holding onto the trauma to prove a point**

A long traumatic experience will shape you in some way. So it happens that there's an identity that is formed around your trauma. You may hesitate to let go. You think it shows that the person who hurt you didn't hurt you as much as you say they did. You think forgiveness will show others that what the person did wasn't all that bad in the first place since you have managed to forgive them. People will never know how deep the trauma runs. They won't understand what it took to reach a point where you had to let go. The damage done changed your whole life. But all they will see is the outcome. They will never know the sleepless nights. They never saw the times you were angry that it happened to you. All they will see is the part where you finally forgave and moved on. Because of that, they will think it was easy for you. It was nowhere close to easy.

A gentle reminder that you don't need to prove to others that what the abuser did hurt you by holding onto the trauma. Holding onto the trauma is more damaging than the point you are trying to prove to others. You are the one who went through the abuse. You are the only one who knows how much it has affected or is affecting you, and that's enough. Trying to prove a point to others makes you stagnant. It distracts you from your feelings and how far you've come. You don't need to prove anything to anyone else. Most of the time, the people you are trying to prove to are actually the ones who have no benefit to you on your journey. You wouldn't have to prove anything to them if they believed you in the first place. Those aren't the type of people you need to be proving anything to. In fact, don't bother with proving your pain to anyone else. You carrying the pain yourself is painful enough. You may try to show people that the abuser really did hurt you, and it's killing you every day. But people still may not understand and may brush you off. Find comfort in knowing that the feelings you have because of the trauma are valid. God knows your story, you know your story, and that's all that matters. At the end of the day, you wouldn't have to prove a point if they understood and listened to you.

## Pro's of forgiving

It's true that forgiveness never changes the situation. It can only change the situation if the person wants to change. But that's okay because forgiveness changes you. It changes something in you. It creates this new life for you; it marks a new beginning and a fresh start within yourself.

Forgiveness is the base for everything. It's like a seed. It needs to be planted first before other parts start to grow. Once you deal with unforgiveness, other parts of your life and healing journey will fall into place more easily.

## How to know if you have forgiven

It's hard to know if you have truly forgiven someone. The best way to check is by looking at what the bible says about forgiveness. When you don't do this, you can trick yourself into falling for your opinion of forgiveness, which sometimes isn't as accurate as you may think. Proverbs 24v17 says, "Don't gloat when your enemy falls; when they stumble, do not let your heart rejoice."

To know if you have truly forgiven the person who hurt you, check your heart posture. How would you feel if something terrible happened to them? Would you be happy? Would you say things like,' Oh, they deserve it anyway?' That is how you know if you have truly forgiven.

Forgiveness is an act of love not just towards other people but towards yourself. You've got to decide to forgive the person who hurt you, not because they deserve it but because you do. You deserve the peace. You deserve happiness, and sometimes, you must do what's best for you to get it. Forgive them for you because, at the end of the day, you are the only one hurt. The best thing you can do for yourself is to do whatever will give you peace, even if that includes stepping out of your comfort zone.

**Julie's story**

I was sexually abused. It made me angry at my family. This caused many arguments, especially with my half-brother. He was the abuser. While I was going through stuff, people were being mean to me in school. I became angry at the world and I struggled with forgiving people a lot. I still struggle but it's like it's getting a lot easier now. It's very hard, but when I started my relationship with God, it became a thing where it's like, okay, you know, I can't have hate in my heart. I still see people and have anger towards them because of what they did to me. It was very hard for me to forgive people, especially when you see them all happy and remember all the sadness they caused you. Now I know the same way God forgives me; I have to forgive other people. My experience with forgiveness has been very hard! Forgiving people has removed much hate from my heart. It has brought me peace. Now, I can view people's social media pages without anger. Now, I just look at them and feel bad for them, and I'm not saying that in a shady way. I'm saying I feel bad for them because I know they could be a lot happier if they had God in their life.

# Vulnerability

It's very hard to define vulnerability because there is no exact definition. Different people will have different definitions depending on their experiences. One thing all can agree on is that vulnerability is exposing a part you wouldn't usually expose. It requires moving away from your comfort zone and expressing your innermost feelings. Vulnerability can look like sharing details of your personal story and its impact on you. It can also look like telling your peers what you got in your exam results. These are two very different scenarios. But each exposes some information. In these examples, there's also stepping out of one's comfort zone. Not everyone will think sharing their exam results is a big deal. It's all a matter of perspective. It's about why someone doesn't share that information and how they feel when they are sharing it. The student who shares their exam results may not be used to doing so. They may also have a deeper reason why they don't share it. By exposing their results, you are being let into a part of their life few have access to.

Being vulnerable changes depending on what your comfort zone is. People's views on vulnerability depend on what they are exposing and their comfort level. It's all perspective, and it changes between me and you. If the situation requires you to speak from a naked point of view and in a very raw way, then that's vulnerability. It's not what you say; it's about how you feel saying that thing. That is the determiner of whether you are being vulnerable or not.

**It's a weak thing to do**

Vulnerability is mostly seen as negative. Most see it as being weak and insecure. It's not true, but it's normal to have a negative outlook. It's especially so if you have tried to express your feelings and got dismissed instead. They responded in a way that shut you down instead of acknowledging what you were opening up about. In the future, this can make you feel weak. It may feel like you've given a part of yourself away without receiving anything in return.

I remember the first time I opened up about my story and told one of my family members what had been happening to me. After the conversation, I immediately regretted it. Their response wasn't something I was expecting. Automatically, I felt weak because I thought that was how they saw me. It felt like someone else had a piece of me but didn't pay the price of getting it by showing me sympathy. From that day on, I decided I would never share my story again. I thought if I did, I would get a response like the one I got from my family members.

**Emotionally unavailable parents**

Having emotionally unavailable parents meant having parents who ignored your emotional needs. They didn't create the safe environment you needed. When you tried to express your feelings, they may have silenced you. The reactions you got may have made you hesitant to open up again. It could also be that your parents did create the space. But, it was crowded with other things. Like them criticising you or making your feelings about themselves.

How caregivers respond to your emotions reflects their own struggles. If they don't deal with their traumas, they carry old, painful emotions. It's unfair that they take them out on you. Emotionally unavailable parents don't realise their words can hurt deeply.

Constantly hearing things like

'You are too young to be depressed,'

'What do you know about depression?'

'How can you feel like that?

'Do you know what I am going through myself?'

Phrases like these brush you off, making you feel like your problems aren't worth the impact they have on you. They do this because they don't know how to respond to your trauma. They never had a vulnerable parent and always had to survive. They aren't able to empathise because they are distant and avoidant with their own emotions. Hence, they expect you to be the same with yours. Other times, they selfishly do this so they can be seen, too. There's nothing wrong with wanting to be seen. It's just about the way you go about it. Trying to be seen shouldn't involve shutting someone else down.

The events you saw in your childhood home can make you walk on eggshells when expressing yourself. You want to avoid hurting your parents' feelings, so you tiptoe on what you say. Anything that affects you as a child will affect you as an adult unless you choose to deal with it. When you don't deal with your past, you may try not to be a burden. So, you avoid the spotlight. You make sure that you make nothing about yourself, so you are kind of hidden away from everyone else.

**Always being seen as a strong friend.**

The strong friend in the group is always there for others, but not for themselves. They are seen as people who don't have problems. If they have problems, they seem to deal with and overcome them well. The strong friend goes above and beyond for everyone because that's what they wish they could do for themselves. If you're a strong friend, it can be uncomfortable to talk to your other friends about your problems. You have already set this image of being hardcore, which you don't want to ruin. It can also feel weird being seen as a weak person when, most days, you seem like you are the one who's always conquering. Joseph in the Bible is a good example of someone many may view as 'strong.' This man had gone through a lot, from being sold as a slave to going to prison for something he didn't do. The Bible doesn't describe how he felt during these challenging times. The Bible only mentions Joseph's emotions when he is the king of Egypt and sees his youngest brother. This part of the story is very emotional. Many see Joseph as a strong person who goes through a lot and always comes out fine. This isn't something you would expect to see from Joseph. This part of the story shows his emotions. They reveal that he was affected more than we as readers know. That's how it works for the strong friend as well.

It will get to a point where they break down. It will shock you because you never thought they were struggling. After all, they never displayed any signs of struggle. That's why strong friends suffer the most: they fight battles on their own. This is a gentle reminder to you that breaking the 'strong friend character' doesn't make you look weak. It means you are brave enough to allow people to see a side of you that you are so scared to reveal.

### Not being acknowledged as a child

There's a phrase that says, 'Children should be seen, not heard.' Unfortunately, this was the harsh reality for most of us growing up, but even worse. You may have grown up in places where you weren't seen or heard. It was like you were invisible. You were just in the background of the people in your life. It became normal because this is all you saw. So, when it's time to be acknowledged, it overwhelms you because it's a first-time thing for you. It's way too out of your comfort zone. So you would do anything to avoid that moment. You will suppress your emotions, lie to others that you are okay, or lie to yourself. Ignoring your feelings causes them to pile up. Your actions then reflect those unexpressed, unresolved feelings. Over time, it starts to make you someone you are not.

### Importance of vulnerability

There are many doors which are locked due to a lack of vulnerability. There are relationships and changes in your lives determined by your vulnerability. Not allowing yourself to be vulnerable makes you lose out on raw moments. A great example of this is Joseph's story when he finally gets to see his youngest brother, Benjamin. He misses his brother so much, and when he sees him, he gets emotional about it. Instead of acting on those feelings and hugging him, he held back his tears. Then, he went to a private room to cry and let it all out. So when he came out of the inner room, he looked like he didn't cry at all. Joseph will see his brother again, but it won't be the same as when he first saw him. His bottling up his emotions made him miss out on this moment.

**Advice**

Vulnerability needs a safe place. You can't just be vulnerable to anyone. You may have people you trust but don't trust them enough to give them access to specific parts of your life. The only guaranteed safe place is God. He will never judge you for how you feel, and He will never overlook your situation. He will never tell you that you are being too dramatic. He's got you. If you need an example of vulnerability, you can look at Job's story. Job told God everything, how he felt. He let God know that, if possible, he would curse the day he was born and wished he didn't exist. You see, Job couldn't do that with anyone; he couldn't do it with his friends to be more specific. That was okay because Job knew he had a safe place to be vulnerable. You also have God as your safe place to be vulnerable. Alongside this, you need to learn how to be vulnerable and honest with yourself. Once you can do that, you are one step closer to being vulnerable to anyone else. It starts with you.

**1. Understand where the fear stems from.**

**Your past experiences**

Knowing where your fear comes from is the first step to overcoming it. Take a closer look and explore your past experiences. That's where you will find the reasons behind your fear of being vulnerable. Consider the times you were rejected or betrayed by someone you loved. Even the moments of small things that had a severe emotional impact on you. Hurtful memories of rejection and betrayal create a fear of opening up to others. These experiences led you to build a wall around yourself as a defence mechanism.

Acknowledging your past and the role it plays in your fears can help you overcome them.

**Acknowledge your emotions**

It's okay to feel scared or anxious about opening up. Fear and anxiety are common emotions that can come up when you're about to open up to someone. The feelings are stronger when you are talking about a life-changing experience. But here's the thing: accepting these emotions goes a long way. Not criticising yourself for having them eases the burden, making it easier to face them. You learn to deal with your emotions and not to beat yourself up for having them. This builds comfort and confidence. For example, think about a time you built up the courage to open up to someone you trust. Once you had opened up, didn't it feel like a weight had been lifted off your shoulders? That's because accepting your emotions lets you process them in a healthy way.

**2. Start small**

**Share in stages**

You don't need to reveal your deepest secrets right away. Start by sharing small, less personal things with someone you trust. As you gain confidence, you can slowly open up more. As you become more comfortable, you can share slightly more personal stories. For example, a funny childhood memory or a challenge you are currently facing. Remember, it's like peeling the layers of an onion—you don't have to expose everything at once. With time and practice, you'll grow more comfortable sharing your thoughts and feelings. Eventually, you'll be ready to reveal more personal parts of yourself.

**Start with the people you already trust**

Begin with people who have shown they are trustworthy. This could be a close friend, family member, or mentor who has shown empathy to you in the past. A safe, supportive environment makes it easier to be vulnerable.

### 3. Changing your perspective on vulnerability

**Vulnerability isn't a weakness.**

It's portrayed that when you are vulnerable, you are weak, when that's not the case. Being vulnerable requires bravery, which goes to show it's actually a strength. It can deepen your relationships with others and yourself. The deepest wounds allow for the deepest healing. Your vulnerability will help you heal and develop a stronger sense of who you are.

### 4. Practice self-compassion

#### Be gentle with yourself

When you open up and share your true feelings, it's natural to feel naked and exposed. Remember, it's normal to feel scared or uneasy when sharing a painful memory. Practising self-compassion is a wonderful way to navigate these uncomfortable emotions. Being kind to yourself will help you build a more gentle and supportive inner voice. It will encourage you to take risks and celebrate small wins along the way.

#### It doesn't have to be perfect

Part of being vulnerable is accepting that you might not always have the right words to say or the ideal reaction in every situation. That's okay. Embracing imperfection makes vulnerability easier. Letting go of perfection helps you stay true to yourself, which can lead to deeper, more authentic relationships.

**5. Focus on the present:**

**Let go of the fear of judgement.**

Often, the fear of vulnerability comes from worrying about how others will react or what they will think. Instead, focus on the present and not the potential of what could happen. Sharing can deepen your connection with others.

**Let go of past rejection.**

Holding onto past hurts can be like carrying heavy baggage that weighs you down. It makes taking that first step into forming new relationships really hard, as betrayal hurts. It can mould your perception of relationships and make you afraid to be vulnerable again. Those past experiences belong to a different chapter of your life. Writing down your feelings is a great way to work through them and release the emotional burdens. Separating past experiences from the present helps you see what's possible now. It distinguishes between what happened then and what's possible now.

### 6. Building emotional resilience

**Accept that vulnerability involves a risk worth taking.**

When you open up to others, there's always a chance they might not respond the way you want them to. This can lead to feelings of disappointment, rejection, or even embarrassment. Being emotionally resilient means handling these situations without shutting down or becoming defensive.

### 7. Set boundaries

**Know your limits:**

Vulnerability isn't a free-for-all. It's not a place to dump your deepest secrets on anyone who will listen. It's about choosing what and with whom to share it. This will help you feel safe and in control. Being open doesn't mean you have to bare your soul to everyone. It means you are willing to be honest with those you trust. For example, you might share your fears with a close friend. But you'd hide them from a work friend. Be mindful of your audience and what you share. It can help you connect more deeply with others while keeping your boundaries. Setting clear boundaries is essential in any kind of relationship. It's okay to say no to sharing certain things if you're not comfortable. Setting boundaries can create a safer place to be vulnerable when you're ready.

Vulnerability can be difficult, but it's a must for real relationships and growth. Take small steps. Be patient and kind to yourself. These can help you slowly overcome your fears and connect more deeply with others.

# LOVE AND TRAUMA

# The partner for you

Manipulation was a big part of the abuse I faced from my father. He was hurting me while convincing me that I was hurting him. When I was 13, I'd tell him I was angry and hated him for what he was doing to me. He would flip the conversation and make me look like a bad person. His constant manipulation made me cautious of everything I did. I didn't want to feel like a bad person or hurt him. Before I knew it, I was walking on eggshells. This was even with people I knew were hurting me. I maintained silence just to keep the peace, but the only peace that was kept was theirs.

There was always this fear that anything I did could hurt someone. When I began to heal from the abuse, I tried to teach myself one thing: if someone mistreats you, it's okay to leave. I had to learn not to feel guilty for speaking up when my feelings were hurt. It wasn't as easy as that because I still felt bad for people who hurt me.

As much as they'd hurt me, I believed they didn't deserve to be told because that meant I was hurting their feelings. I would always put the feelings of the villain over mine. I felt guilty and sorry for them, so I overlooked what they were doing. I couldn't cut them loose. It seemed selfish to put myself first, so I let them get away with it. Those feelings came from years of manipulation when I was made to feel like the bad person for talking about what was hurting me. It really stuck with me, and without knowing it, I carried this on into my early adulthood as well. I never understood why I would feel bad for doing what was good for me. I didn't understand why I felt bad for cutting ties with people who were hurting me.

It was only when I started healing that things became clearer. I realised it was a bigger issue than I thought. Knowing why you do certain things is good, but it's even better when you know how to break that cycle.

## You are attracted to what you have experienced

One fun fact about the brain is that it thinks in images and is attracted to what it sees. For example, let's say you want to buy a specific shoe. Before you decide to buy that shoe, you never saw it anywhere. But now, all of a sudden, when you have decided to buy or even bought the shoe, you are seeing it everywhere. This applies to life experiences too. If you see something often, you will be attracted to it. Your life experiences will mould your preferences, drawing you towards the familiar. So, if you are attracted to anything toxic but need to know exactly where it stems from. Explore your past and look at what you had to witness in your childhood, and that will hint at why your brain is attracted to that toxicity. Looking at your past and diving into your childhood memories will help you pinpoint the roots of harmful attractions.

This attraction can be even in the things you consider to be small. Suppose you experienced manipulation or were given promises that were never fulfilled. In that case, you may find that you are attracted to people who don't stick to their word or aren't sure about you.

You see, the thing with this is that you may have decided to choose someone who is all about you, but what you picked up from childhood will prevail. You go for what's familiar even if it doesn't match what you say you want. The need for comfort leads you back to the same old relationship patterns you saw when you were growing up. If you grew up with inconsistent caregivers, it's like they were there physically but not emotionally. This can move with you when you get older. You may notice that as a result of this, you are easily drawn to partners who are one foot in and one foot out.

**Love and the conscious mind**

It's common to get drawn to the same type of love you saw growing up, even if it wasn't healthy. If you saw your parents always arguing you might be attracted to a partner who always argues even though you want a peaceful relationship. It gets to a point where you have your own new standard but still go for the opposite of what you truly desire. Your conscious mind knows what you want in a relationship. It knows the standard you have, but your subconscious doesn't know that. Your subconscious will be stuck on autopilot. It will repeat the patterns you saw in your childhood until it learns something different. When you only see dysfunction, you will run on the toxicity. You will do this until you learn a better way to love.

To change how you love and who you love, your brain needs to be rewired. You need to learn a new way of loving so you don't keep falling into the same old patterns of your childhood. This can be especially challenging if you grew up in a household where dysfunction was the norm. You may discover that you are caught in a pattern of unhealthy relationships. That's why it's always important to reflect on your decisions. This pattern only changes when you first notice and know that the pattern is there for a reason. Then, the next step is diving back into your childhood to see the root of the pattern. Doing this helps bring the things that are hidden in the subconscious to the surface. After that, you can then start unlearning the toxicity your childhood still holds on you. The more you unlearn, the more you start to embrace what truly fulfils you. Also, being self-aware and noticing when you are about to repeat a pattern can help. If you catch yourself in the moment and decide to act differently, it can break harmful cycles. Over time, with constant renewing of

the mind, your actions will start matching what's in your conscious. Finally, there's no hidden information to overpower what's in the conscious.

**Love and your childhood:**

If your childhood needs were neglected, it's likely that, as an adult, you are always trying to meet those unmet needs without realising it. The relationships you get into fail not because you are unlovable. They fail because you seek out dynamics that mirror your childhood. For instance, if you had a parent who was always criticising you, you might end up with a partner who does the same. Or, if you felt neglected when you were a kid, you might keep choosing partners who are unavailable or distant. Your attempts to fulfil unmet childhood needs attract people who mirror those who failed to meet them. When you keep dating different people but get the same result, it shows a pattern that needs to be broken. You're likely doing something the same. Or, there's something they have in common that's attracting you to all these people. Know the pattern is there. Question what it shows about your childhood and your relationships with those responsible for you. Reflecting on your past can help you identify how your unmet childhood needs are affecting your adult relationships. Remember, it takes time to break patterns. It requires self-reflection. But it's a journey worth taking. It can lead to a more meaningful and satisfying life.

**Heal before getting into a relationship**

As someone who had an abusive childhood, I had to constantly swallow my pain to survive. Over time, I grew a high pain tolerance, which meant that it took a lot for you to hurt me. During this stage of my life, if you managed to get to me, it means you would have done a lot for you to get there. This high pain tolerance became a big problem for me, especially when I started getting into relationships.

I had a hard time understanding what healthy relationships looked like. It was hard to figure out what was okay and what wasn't. What other people would consider as unhealthy would be fine to me. For me, it would have taken a relationship to push me to my limit. To completely destroy me and then that's when I would have acknowledged the relationship wasn't good. A relationship needed to consume and shatter me for me to know it's not healthy to be in it. Even with that, I'd find a way to stay.

You see, it's easy to start becoming immune to pain when you have been through the worst already. So when you get into a relationship, someone needs to do a lot to hurt you. This high pain tolerance becomes very dangerous, especially in relationships. Because it means that a relationship will have to get so toxic that you will feel the pain of being in it. On top of that, it takes a lot to leave a relationship, even when it's unbearable to stay in. Yet, you still find a way to survive through it.

Having a trauma-free childhood helps spot toxic relationships more quickly. People who didn't face trauma often sense when something is off in their relationships faster. They don't stay until the relationship crushes them but leave when they see warning signs. Childhood trauma survivors often have a hard time spotting toxic relationships. They've learned to handle a lot of pain, which can make them overlook unhealthy signs. Since they're used to feeling hurt, they might think that's what love feels like. This can keep them stuck in bad relationships, making their trauma worse. So they wait until the relationship turns toxic and reaches a point of no return to realise it's enough. You have to get pushed to your maximum in order for you to know that maybe you should walk away. Lowering your pain tolerance will give you the power to know when to let go, so you don't need to be pushed to the maximum to acknowledge that you need to leave. Heal before getting into a relationship. Then, continue working on yourself as you continue in the relationship. Healing isn't a destination; it's a journey.

### Tolerating what you wouldn't if you knew your value

Trauma changes everything about your life. It makes you settle in places and relationships you wouldn't have if you hadn't gone through what you did. Love is a big area affected by trauma. Often, how you were cared for as a child spills into your future love life. People who went through child abuse were often neglected and received inconsistency from their parents. The effects of this are so deep because it leaves them lonely with this empty void that can't seem to be filled. It goes without saying that when they get older, there is this constant search for something to fill that void they have had for so long. There's this desperate need for them to receive what their parents didn't give them as kids.

Being desperate isn't always good because it leads to settling for less. Having this craving for love means some settle for toxic forms of it. When you never received love growing up, any sort of love will be good as long as you receive it. The thing about the love you settle for when you are desperate is that it will always force you to compromise. One of the biggest compromises is your well-being. If you compromise on your well-being, you compromise your whole life. If you have noticed when your mental state isn't in a good place, everything else in your life will feel like it's falling apart. That's why you can never compromise on your well-being. The consequences of dating the wrong person are far-reaching. They don't just affect the relationship but the overall quality of your life.

I was someone who had a very misleading perception of love. I was afraid of the love that was good for me, and I always settled for relationships that were bad for me. I thought my view of love was normal at first, but that all changed when I experienced God's love for me. By reading the word of God and seeing what He says about me and how much He loves me, my perception of love started to alter. I thought I was only able to understand what true love is when the love of my life comes and shows it to me. But that wouldn't have happened if nothing changed. My fear of love would have pushed him away before I could experience it. Your perception of love is built based on what you witnessed from the people caring for you while growing up. When you are used to having a chaotic childhood, it makes it hard to go for a gentle love. Your current perception of love will change once you experience what real love is.

**The three attachment styles**

There are three different attachment styles—secure, anxious, and avoidant. The secure attachment style is ideally the attachment style everyone wants. But abuse and maltreatment from your caregivers block you from being securely attached. A secure attachment style in childhood comes from consistent, loving caregivers. When those responsible for you neglected or abused you, things like trust issues were created instead. If you don't develop a secure attachment, you become either avoidantly or anxiously attached. Anxiety and avoidance are opposites. An anxiously attached person will do the opposite of an avoidant person. There are many signs of what an avoidant attachment style will look like. Two of them being when you are overly independent and pushing relationships away when they get close. Overly self-reliant people fear being let down by others. They were hurt by their caregivers, so to avoid that pain, they learnt to depend only on themselves. As children, the pain of unmet needs was unbearable. Now, to avoid that pain, you try to protect yourself. You do this by distancing yourself when relationships get too close.

**God sent v devil sent**

The way to know if a relationship is from God or the devil is by looking to see if there's a compromise. Compromises aren't harmful. They are only bad when forced to compromise areas you shouldn't. The partner God sends will never cause you to compromise, let alone make you feel confused about being with them in the first place. There's reassurance when the thing is from God but confusion when it's from the devil. It will be hard to discern the things of God and the things of the enemy simply because these compromises aren't always as loud as you think. You need to watch out for these compromises that way; if the relationship is sent your way, even if it may look good at a glance, you will know it's not for you. When the devil tried to tempt Jesus, he used compromises. He made everything look like what God would say, but he included his own twist, which made it a compromise. When the devil tried his tricks on Jesus, it didn't work because Jesus went back and referenced what God said. He did that to show that who the devil's sends may look like they are from God. It will only seem that way when you don't know God's standard in the first place. Overlooking the compromise is easy when the relationship looks so good. At first it looks minor but as time goes by it becomes harder to tolerate it. The person who isn't for you will always look like a mimicked version of who God will send. You will know they aren't the one through the compromise. Compromises can be good but this specific compromise will be in a certain area of your life you shouldn't compromise.

**The partner who isn't good for you**

The strategy the devil uses to try to tempt Jesus is the same tactic he uses nowadays. The Bible mentions that after the failure to tempt Him, the devil waited again for an opportune time to tempt Jesus. The devil isn't powerful enough to get to you when you are at your best, so he always waits for an opportune time. He waits for the moments of defeat, emptiness, or when there's a craving for love. He knows it's in these moments when you are desperate that you will take anything offered. So that's when he sends you partners who aren't yours. Partners who send you back to where you are trying to come from. His main goal is to keep you hurting. So, he will always send you someone who puts you in a worse place. Better believe toxic relationships are his best tactic for this.

When love was limited in your childhood, and you didn't feel genuine love, that affects your future love life. The consequence may be that you are attracted to individuals whose intentions with you are just to use you while showing you a sprinkle of love. This is also known as breadcrumbing.

It's when someone gives you just enough love and attention for you to stay, whilst giving you too little to be satisfied.

In situations like these, you may know that how you are being treated by the person isn't good, but you tolerate it. So, a fear springs up when a person who wants to genuinely take care of you makes it very clear they don't want to use you. Because a part of you believes that every guy who comes into your life has already decided they don't want you for you. However, the ones who won't use you are the ones you are sceptical about because of the lack of genuine love in your childhood. Choosing the right partner for you will always be determined by how you see yourself. How you love yourself will decide who you choose to have access to you. When you don't see yourself as someone who's truly deserving of love in a healthy way, you will give chances to people who do nothing but walk all over you. But once you know how precious you are, you will move according to that. It will always start with you.

**The feeling of love isn't enough**

It's okay to want to feel loved, but remember settling for someone just because they make you feel loved isn't enough. It won't be enough if everything else they are doing contradicts the love they are showing you. Love isn't just about how the person makes you feel; it's also about how they treat and react towards you when things aren't going great. It's everything their actions show. I know you may want to feel what love feels like, but trust me, settling for a part-time type of love isn't worth it because you will be left hurting again after it. Love is consistent. God set the standard for you and shows that love isn't just a one-time thing.

You deserve way better than the tiny fragments of love you are receiving. Depending on what you went through, it's easy to feel like no-one out there will ever love you. But, let me burst that thought. Someone out there will love you more than you expect. There's someone who will do more than give you the feeling of love. There's someone out there who won't enhance your insecurities but will instead push you to be your best. Work on yourself, and don't let your insecurities be the reason why you open the door of love. That way, you won't go for a bare minimum type of love because you now know what you truly deserve.

# Fear of Intimacy

People with an avoidant attachment style dodge emotional closeness. This comes from a deep-rooted fear of getting hurt or being abandoned. They may come across as not wanting intimacy. They might come off as standoffish, not wanting hugs or intimate moments. But they're torn between wanting a connection and fearing it. They keep their emotions distant while hoping someone will reach out. Avoidant individuals want closeness and intimacy, but only when it suits them. They play it safe, getting near when they feel comfortable, then backing off when they don't. This back-and-forth game harms their relationships. It shows their struggle to connect while wanting to protect themselves. With avoidant people, a part of them still wants a connection or intimacy, but there's a fear of it.

When you first meet someone, conversations are usually surface-level. As you build stronger bonds, the intimacy increases. That means being vulnerable is needed. For someone with an avoidant attachment style, this stage feels unsafe. People with avoidant attachment have learned to suppress their emotions. Their past makes it hard for them to trust others or form close bonds. Trust is something that they can't grasp, so they push people away before they hurt them again. Intimacy and vulnerability create unease. The more you share about yourself, the greater your discomfort will grow. The more you open up, the more anxious you get, and to overcome it, the anxiety demands you to open up even more.

Past betrayal still lingers, making it tough for you to trust again. Even if the person you are talking to bears no blame for old wounds. Fear will always sneak in as a reminder of when someone broke your trust. This fear isn't a reflection of your current relationship but rather about the memories of past pain. Relying on others puts you at risk of being hurt, and being let down opens wounds. Unconsciously, you learn to guard your heart because trusting means risking more hurt. So, you try to avoid this at all costs by creating a distance between you and your romantic partner. This distance becomes your safe place now. Staying close but also far enough from them so their actions won't have an effect on you.

Not being used to being cared for can make you feel uneasy about affection at first. Kindness might be a new thing, and that makes you wonder what the hidden agenda behind their nice actions is. This keeps you on the lookout, wondering and waiting to pinpoint why they're being so nice. Building deep connections is hard especially when you're used to people not caring. When someone shows real care, it's hard to believe it's genuine. It almost feels like a trap has been created to be used to hurt you. As things get serious, you naturally pull back because you don't feel safe. The track record of painful memories hangs around, telling you to keep people at arm's length.

**Pauline's story**

I didn't realise I was avoidant until a friend pointed it out. After reflecting on this, I saw a pattern in all the people and relationships I had engaged in. I talked to different people but always got the same outcome. Before I would usually point the finger at my boyfriends as if to say they were the reason why the relationship wasn't working. Not realising I was flaw-finding. I was finding their flaws so I could distance myself from the potential of being the problem. I justified my unavailability and lack of vulnerability by pointing out their wrongs. Convincing myself the relationship didn't work because of them made me feel better. I focused on finding their flaws to avoid working on the ones in me. I had to hold myself accountable. Admitting I could have played in the relationship not going beyond surface level was hard but necessary. This left me with no choice but to explore what was poisoning my chance at these amazing relationships which could have been formed.

Another day, I remember sitting in the car with one of my friends, talking about life and doing a catch-up, as one does. There, I found myself being vulnerable but feeling the biggest ick and disgust while doing it. It got to a point where I just wanted to get out of the car and run because the thought of being vulnerable made me sick and so nervous. I clearly struggled with vulnerability. I wouldn't open up to anyone even to save my life.

A moment later, my friend got straight to the point and told me I was being avoidant. Then he started to describe everything I do as an avoidant person, leaving me stunned and silent. It was so accurate, almost like he knew me more than I knew myself.

"How do you know that?" I asked with the biggest shock on my face. He then told me about his therapy sessions, where he had been learning about different attachment styles.

I was too shocked at what I was hearing because I was like, damn, that all makes sense now. It was weird. Someone was telling me about my relationships, yet they didn't know anything about my love life. Everything made sense. It was like he solved the puzzle of my relationship life without me even telling him anything. I wanted a healthy relationship. So, I read books and watched videos about avoidant attachment styles. I hoped to one day finally stop being this way. As I went on, it became clear there was no cheat code to fix my ways. I needed to explore my past to find the root of the issue.

I had a comforting relationship with my father before coming to terms with the fact that what my father was doing was abusive. I was naive then, so I saw him as perfect. I knew I could rely on him for everything. I knew that if the world ended, he would be the first person I would go to. I knew that he had my best interest at heart. I was so overprotective of him that I would have done anything for him because I loved him so much. Most of my feelings towards him changed once I realised what he was doing to me wasn't right, and it was intentional.

I began to see that the one I'd lay everything down for was the one who didn't care about hurting me. I felt so many emotions as a child, but I couldn't express them. I was ashamed of what would happen if everyone knew what was going on behind closed doors. After the abuse stopped, I subconsciously chose to never feel the same pain my father caused me.

I did everything to protect myself from feeling hurt again. My avoidant self was a protection. It was a way of making sure that no one ever had access and power to hurt me like that again. That meant I never allowed relationships to reach a point further than the surface level. With a relationship being surface level, I knew that any pain from it would be minimal because I hadn't invested too much into it. I ran away from relationships when they got too intimate. I had understood that if I cared for someone the same way I did for my father, then I'd be hurt all over again.

## Am I avoidant?

Doing everything and being very self-reliant is a sign of the avoidant attachment style. This is the consequence of having no one to turn to but yourself. You have had no one to turn to but yourself all your life. You've learnt to trust yourself because you rarely let yourself down. When someone you trust betrays you, it hurts like crazy. The pain goes deep and leaves scars that can make you wary of getting close to others again. You start seeing threats everywhere, even when they're not real. It's natural to want to protect yourself from getting hurt again, but building walls around yourself can backfire. Instead of avoiding harm, they can keep out the good stuff, like connection and happiness. Facing abuse tears your life apart in so many different ways. It destroys your trust, leaving you feeling unsafe and vulnerable. The wounds it forms affect every area of your life, making it hard to recover.

## How did we get here?

Avoidant behaviour comes from constant hurt and betrayal by those who should have protected and loved you.

If your primary caregiver was someone you loved, but they rejected your love, you would likely become scared to show it again. Letting your guard down can be very scary, making it feel like a big risk to fall in love again. This kind of hurt can stick with you for a long time, affecting how you handle relationships even after you've moved on from the original hurt. Being able to trust the people who were supposed to protect you was so important. Your home is one place that's supposed to be your safe haven. But when the people who were supposed to keep you safe and care for you were untrustworthy. Every day would have been a fight to feel safe, loved and seen. Your caregivers were supposed to be the ones who could be counted on, and when that wasn't the case, it played with you as a child. Betrayal from those who should love you hurts, and it can get you to a point where you are fed up and can't afford to endure any more pain and trauma.

Your childhood plays a big role in how you love. Feeling safe and loved as a kid makes you better at creating strong relationships. But when you are forced to survive tough times, it is harder to get close to others later on. What happens when you are a child shapes a lot of who you are and how you connect with people as you grow up. If your childhood involved abuse from someone close to you, there will always be a fear attached to love, which makes you not show it or receive it.

You link love with hurt, so when you are shown love, you find it hard to accept it and prepare for the worst. It's a real battle letting people in. Deep down, there's this belief that love will always equal heartbreak.

**Pauline's story**

My father used to do loving acts; he used to buy me stuff and treat me like a princess. To me, I felt special, and I felt appreciated. When the abuse started, I understood that these gestures weren't genuine and were only done to his benefit. I noticed that his 'loving acts' came with a price. As I grew older and could start dating, I was always wary of anyone who did something nice or offered to help me. The genuine act of kindness from the guys I talked to signalled that they wanted something from me. I was baffled at the fact that people could be kind without wanting anything. To make it worse, I couldn't comprehend that someone could be nice to me without wanting to hurt me. The goal was to work on removing this shell, which protected me from the false idea that everyone would hurt me again and that no one would love me for me.

Sometimes, people will hurt you. That's a part of life, but not everyone who enters your life hides under a mask. Some people are genuinely nice. By facing my biggest fear, I proved that good people exist.

**Hyper independence**

One thing about betrayal is that it can come from anyone, even the people you least expect it from. Betrayal hurts like crazy when it's someone you trust. You will feel disappointed and start to question your ability to make good decisions. The catalyst for the betrayals isn't that you made a bad decision. You trusted their intentions, and it's a shame they went against who they showed themselves to be. At the end of the day, you didn't think they could betray you. The bitter feeling of being lied to stays, making it hard to trust others or even yourself. You can't bear the pain of being let down again. Those bad memories leave a mark, reminding you that relying on others isn't safe. Deciding to only depend on yourself isn't something you do while knowing it. When you don't have trust, you've got no choice but to rely on yourself. You start building your independence because you have to.

**Fear of abandonment**

Childhood hurts shape how you think about love and relationships as adults, making you see everything through a lens of fear. The pain of not being loved or supported can echo throughout your whole life, affecting every romantic relationship you have. Fear of being alone makes you cling to relationships way too tightly. You become scared of being abandoned, and that's because of the lack of love from your parents when you were a kid.

Getting into a relationship and a partner becomes distant brings all those old hurt feelings back. It's like reliving your childhood all over again. You feel the original pain of the past without being in the situation that caused it. Being scared of being alone makes you cling to anything to escape the loneliness. You may cling to harmful bonds full of red flags not by choice but to fill an inner void.

**Advice**

If your childhood needs were unmet, you may not realise it, but you are always trying to meet those needs in your adult relationships. Your heart is still hurt from past trauma, and it's hard to accept real love. Instead, you go for what's familiar - a messed-up version of love based on your childhood wounds. So your relationships fail not because you're unlovable. It's because you are seeking relationship dynamics that resemble those you had in your childhood. Recognise the patterns in the relationships you get and see which broken part of your childhood they point to. If you aren't aware of something, you will never know to change it. That's why noticing the patterns is good for you; you know which part of you they are reflecting on and can then work on that part. Getting into any relationship to fill a void only deepens the emptiness within. When they fail, they leave you feeling emptier and worse off than when you started. To find true satisfaction in your relationships, first, be satisfied with yourself.

The Bible says that God is love. It doesn't say that God shows love. It literally says that God defines love because He is what love is. When I felt God's love, things changed. Nothing was ever the same again. At a point in my life, I was itching for love. I really needed it because after the abuse started, I felt hated by my father, and I felt hated by myself. Once, I felt God's love for me, everything changed because He taught me that no love will ever compare to His love for me. Most importantly, the love I received when I was younger isn't what true love was despite it being all I saw. God's love for you is the most genuine love you will ever experience. You better know that when you get to know God more, you will get to know you. You can get to know God more by simply spending more time with him through prayer and reading His word. Getting to know who He is will teach you who He is to you.

# FAMILY & TRAUMA

# Breaking the silence

Breaking the silence means speaking up about a sensitive topic that has been suppressed for a long time. For once, you finally get the chance to say what's been happening behind closed doors. It's time for the hidden truth to come out and a weight lifted off your shoulders. This is the real turning point where you release the emotional burdens you have carried. Raw emotions flood to the surface when you revisit a painful memory. Your layer of protection drops and suddenly you feel exposed. This makes you vulnerable and fearful of what others might think of your experiences. The discomfort comes from your deepest worries, where you've kept your emotional scars hidden for so long. It's scary to be vulnerable when talking about a trauma. If you grew up hiding your feelings to seem strong, you know how true this is. It is the beginning of your healing journey. For the first time, you realise you're not isolated in your struggle. As you express your emotions, you slowly break free and find your voice, which is normally lost after facing a traumatic event. Depending on your support system, you can get comfort and empathy from those around you.

**Pauline's story**

The abuse coming from my biological father made it harder for me to speak up. I feared what people would think of me afterwards. I was more worried about people's opinions simply because people viewed my father as some sort of superhero. I had a huge doubt that whoever I broke the silence to was going to believe me. They wouldn't have thought he was the type of father to hurt his daughter the way he did. I debated whether to break the silence. But I soon found the courage to speak the truth about what had been happening. For once in 6 years, someone else got to know the pain that this little girl had been carrying along by herself. It wasn't all roses and petals though. Some family members I opened up to made me feel blamed for the situation. It was clear to me the perpetrator was in the wrong. So, I struggled to understand how they didn't see that too.

A couple of weeks after breaking the silence, I have to say that I regretted it. I all of a sudden became the gossip of the family. My insecurities didn't help with this situation either. I knew that every time my family saw me, they would think of what I'd told them. On a few occasions, they would ask ignorant questions. I had to give them the benefit of the doubt and assume good intent in their questions. But I would be lying if I said my heart didn't sink each time they asked me such things. I began to normalise their ignorance. It may be because they hadn't gone through it, and that's why they didn't know how to approach this. Breaking my silence was supposed to be freeing. But, after breaking it, I felt more shamed and cast away by my family. Though I didn't get the support I needed, breaking the silence taught me a lesson I couldn't have learned otherwise. At the end of it all, breaking the silence was a blessing in disguise for me. It showed me the people that don't need to come with me on this journey of healing from the trauma.

Breaking the silence will do you more harm than good when it's to the wrong people. You lose a lot of family when you finally start to find your voice. Most family members want to hide what happened to protect their image. They try to do this by silencing you. The hardest pill to swallow is that things may never be the same with your family after you break your silence. The thought of that is painful, especially when the people involved are people you love and trust. Remember, the people you lost when you found your voice aren't a loss. When you lose family members who dismiss your pain, you aren't losing anything. God is just removing the unnecessary people you won't need on this journey. You can't afford to take unsupportive, dismissive people as you heal from trauma. That will only create a deeper wound. So remember that being alone is better than being surrounded by people who never believed you when you told the truth. When the journey gets lonely (because it will), remember that the loneliness is for a period. God is with you, guiding you. He'll help you find life's true meaning away from the trauma your family caused you.

### Choosing the side of the abuser

Family members often side with the abuser, leaving the victim to face the situation alone. Depending on your family setting, speaking up usually doesn't get you much support. Instead, relatives quietly take the perpetrator's side, downplaying or dismissing your pain. This betrayal makes the original hurt even worse. The thing about child perpetrators is that they mask themselves a lot. When the silence breaks about a family member, there's often shock. It's hard to believe the accused person did it, given who they have been pretending to be. It's hard for people to accept because the person they knew would never do something like that. They either find it hard to believe you. Or, if they do, they don't see the person as a threat despite it being revealed that the person isn't who they thought after all. They make the abuser look like the victim and focus on understanding what drove them rather than how their actions hurt you.

## Reasons why it's hard to break the silence

**Having so much yet nothing to say**

This happens when a lot has happened to you but has never been talked about. The weight of unspoken experiences becomes crushing. When you finally talk about these things, you can become overwhelmed with how much there is to share. There's so much to say but no clear place to start. You become lost for words and feel like you have nothing to say when really there's too much to say.

**Not used to speaking about your problems.**

Breaking your silence means giving someone access to a large part of your life. It's harder to break the silence when that's not something you're used to doing. This vulnerability can be unsettling. It's worse if you have maintained silence for so long. It's natural to fear allowing someone to enter the secrets of your past.

**You feel ashamed and don't want to look like a victim.**

The experience of whatever you have been going through has made you a victim enough. Opening up will require you to be vulnerable, which you wouldn't want to do because you feel like vulnerability also makes you a victim. You don't want to let your strong girl guard down. On top of this, you could feel ashamed, not because of what happened. When the abuser is someone you had or were supposed to have a close relationship with, it can be hard to break the silence. One reason is the shame and embarrassment you will feel, the judgement and whether people will believe you.

## It's okay to cry

Growing up, you may have struggled to cry in front of others because you didn't want to be seen as weak or vulnerable. Instead, you learned how to bottle up your emotions to show your strength and put on a brave face to avoid feeling like a burden. The 'strong' person is always seen as the person who doesn't get affected by anything. What most don't understand is that individuals who appear to have it all together aren't immune to emotional distress. They seem to have their life together. But, they hide struggles and fear that their vulnerability will be seen as a weakness.

They don't show emotion even when they tell the saddest stories, even though deep down, they are broken by the experience. Behind closed doors, they break down, but in front of everyone, they need to look like they have it all together. Remember that allowing yourself to cry takes away the tough exterior that you may have built up as a defence. When you cry, you begin to dive into your emotions and gain a deeper understanding of why you feel the way you do. Tears uncover hidden pain and reveal suppressed emotions. Embracing your tears is the first step towards processing and releasing your emotions.

## Laughter as a coping mechanism

Some people laugh in serious situations. It's not because it's funny. They do it to cope with their discomfort. If the person you are opening up to doesn't get this, they may struggle to empathise with you and see your situation as less severe. Tears and sad faces give hints as to how serious a situation is. So when that's not there, you are less likely to be taken seriously. Some believe that tears and anger are the only ways to show that something has deeply affected them. You might end up laughing or joking while telling your story. Knowing this lowers your expectations of the person who doesn't understand your pain.

## Your expectations & their judgement

Disappointment isn't something you expect when breaking the silence. You assume that, since it's a sensitive topic, it would touch them. You hope they will take a share of your pain. When you trust someone, things don't always go as planned. Sharing your story can backfire and lead to some pretty unexpected reactions. Before breaking your silence, know this: Some won't respond to your story as you expect them to. They may lack the capacity to digest it, or, they may be ignorant and not care enough.

Know that some people lack the capacity to understand your story. Opening up to an ignorant person will make you regret it. You'll end up feeling worse about yourself. A closed-minded person may lack the empathy you need and sometimes may shut you down. It's vital to choose trusted people to whom you can safely break your silence.

It's completely normal to fear that speaking out will lead you to be judged. In some cases, it does happen. Behaviour will always speak louder than words, so an individual may claim they aren't judging you. But their actions will speak for themselves. Breaking the silence when also suffering from depression and anxiety is a big struggle. A fear of being judged makes it even harder. So, I stress the need to talk to someone you trust. Someone you have discussed a sensitive topic with and has shown empathy in their response.

## Asking questions about your story as a source of gossip

Not everyone will know what to say to you when you break your silence to them. Sometimes, people ask thoughtless questions. They want to understand your experience and find the best way to support you, but don't go about it the right way. It's good to be aware when someone is asking questions as a way of looking to understand you better. It's also good to note when someone dives into your experiences, to use what you tell them as a source of gossip. So if someone asks you a question that rubs you the wrong way, it's okay to nudge them and let them know their question is insensitive and dismissive. A person who genuinely cares will apologise and hear you out. A gossip will be offended by what you told them and may make you more uncomfortable.

## Breaking your silence to the perpetrator

Abusers hide their tracks by pretending to have a strong bond with the victim. Many people outside your past relationship may have thought everything was perfect. However, that's not quite the case. The truth is the relationship is not what outsiders think it is. Breaking the silence can be really tough, and you might worry about whether people will believe you. Remember, opening up allows you to find a support system. You're not alone in this, and your feelings are valid.

It's painful enough to have gone through what you did go through that you can't afford to try to convince people that it did happen. A traumatic experience is painful enough. On top of that, trying to convince others it did happen is a heavy burden in itself.

It forces you to relieve the pain all over again but with the added frustration of not being believed. You already have enough pain to deal with. The saddest thing is that people will still question you even when you speak the truth. What matters is that you told the truth.

Remember, when you are breaking your silence, some people won't believe you, but it's not your job to make them. You aren't trying to prove it happened. You are just letting them know it did. That's it.

**Their actions were intentional**

The perpetrator acted in a way that initially made them seem like they weren't thinking about how their actions affected you. Maybe they said or did things that made you think they didn't realise the harm they were causing. But deep down, they knew. This kind of behaviour is common among manipulators who want to control and use others. They hide their true motives, making you question yourself and what you should believe. Being a child at the time, they probably thought you were clueless about how their actions hurt you. So they figured they could get away with treating you badly without you even noticing. What the perpetrator did was crush you, but you were scared to talk to others about it. You worried about what might happen if you did speak out. Now that time has gone, you may decide to confront the perpetrator. Expressing how their actions have hurt you. Showing them the emotional damage they have forced you to carry. They could either show remorse. Or they could make it about themselves. Highlighting how they are the victim and that you are the bad guy.

Often, they will say comments like:

‘Oh, how can you say you hate me?’

‘That’s so rude. You saying you hate me makes me feel sad.’

Comments like these can make you question whether your feelings about the situation are valid. After constant manipulation, you can end up feeling like the bad person instead. Gaslighting and manipulation can make you doubt your sanity. They can rob you of your own mind and leave you thinking you’re the villain in your story. You begin to second-guess your thoughts and feelings, and before you know it, you start to rely on the manipulator for validation.

The effect of gaslighting always reveals itself in your responses to people. You will find it hard to say no even when you want to. Always trying to please others means that turning them down leads to you feeling guilty. Your constant fight against being a bad person means you want to be seen as the opposite of what the manipulator saw you as.

There are many successful stories whereby speaking to the perpetrator has helped the victim. This isn’t to say that you should or shouldn’t be breaking your silence to the perpetrator. However, I advise only talking to the perpetrator if they are willing to do it first. Their willingness to change makes the difference. It shows they know their actions were wrong. From my story, the perpetrator never approached me because they were convinced they weren't doing anything wrong. Everything to them seemed normal. If this is the same or similar case to you, then breaking the silence of the abuser will be the last thing you want to do.

**Blaming your actions on your experiences**

I remember I had erratic behaviour for so many years, and no one ever understood why I was that way. They would often see me as disobedient or cold-hearted. But once they found out, they understood, and it all made sense. It made me feel seen. I sometimes felt crazy and rude for acting a certain way. People looked at me negatively for it. Once everyone knew my story, it gave reasoning for my actions but didn't justify them. My behaviour still remained my responsibility. What happened to me wasn't an excuse to act anyhow. The goal is to notice and be aware of the behaviour and work towards changing that behaviour.

You can't let your past define you forever. I promise you there's so much more on the other side of your trauma. That is always hard to believe, especially since you are currently in it. I struggled with wanting to heal. The abuse stole so much from me. I feared that if I let go of who it had made me, I would be left with nothing. But it always leaves me emotional. After years of living under a dark cloud of depression, I was able to heal from the trauma. I now live a life that's the complete opposite of what I've been through. It goes to show you that there's nothing God won't turn around for you. I don't look like what I've been through, nor does my life. I say that to say healing from past experiences takes hard work. The load is lightened when you allow God to lead your journey. What you will experience on the other side of your trauma is something that can't even compare to what you have been through. I can confidently say that because I have experienced that and know it can happen for you too.

**It's not that deep: invalidating your feelings**

The longer you're stuck in a painful situation, the more the hurt becomes normal. It's like your brain gets used to the pain, and it doesn't feel as serious after a while. The only way to avoid the pain of what happened is to try to downplay and tell yourself it isn't that serious. Masking the pain of the experience also includes invalidating your feelings. It means downplaying the emotions and triggers you have. One of the worst things about trauma is that you go through it while pretending you aren't. And often, you will find you suffer silently, hide your pain and pretend everything is okay even when it's not. What you went through did hurt. You wouldn't need to convince yourself it wasn't that serious if it didn't. You've shown incredible strength by getting this far despite the tough time you have had. I'm sorry you had to go through it. Your feelings about what happened are real, and you're not overreacting. The pain is still there, and it's no wonder you're still hurting. Your emotional response to your pain is valid, and your feelings are not exaggerated.

On some occasions, the brain completely forgets all that happened, and it may all come back to you randomly. The more you speak about what happened, the more you start to remember what happened. Breaking the silence can feel like reliving a nightmare. It can almost feel unreal if the abuse had happened for many years but has never been talked about. But facing the truth is the only way to accept that it really did happen. By acknowledging the past, you can begin to break free from it. Healing starts with a tough truth - you're hurt way worse than you thought. As you start this journey, remember it's okay to need more help than you thought. It's also okay to be vulnerable and ask for that help. I'm rooting for you and sending love as you continue to face your wounds and heal from them.

# Family is everything

I moved from Kenya to London around the age of 9. This was going to be the first time I was going to live with my biological father. I lived with my father alongside other relatives I hadn't met before. From what I remember, my family was like any other. Nothing ever happened that made me question them. All I saw was smiles and people getting along. I didn't notice any fights or drama. I was too innocent, and that made ordinary moments feel like signs of a perfect family. I slowly forgot about Kenya as I settled into this new life, not realising there were issues hiding beneath the surface.

The few months before the abuse started, I saw my father as my best friend. That didn't change even when the abuse started. I loved him so much that I would literally take a bullet for him. Not to be dramatic, but that's what 9-year-old me would tell you. She would tell you she looked up to her father. She wouldn't change him for a different dad, even if you bought her all the dolls in the world. I was so connected to my father that every minor inconvenience he had spilt back to the younger me. I only wanted to see him happy, so even his life problems started to affect me. A few years later, after the abuse had started, I started to resent my father a little. The older I got, the more furious I became. I didn't understand what I had done to make him act that way.

As I approached ages 14 and above, my opinion of my father began to change. My life and emotions were changing so fast that I couldn't keep up. A huge part of me hated him, but another bigger part still loved him deeply. Now, when I look back, I see it wasn't genuine love. It was a way of protecting myself—pretending to care to avoid getting hurt.

Fast forward a few years later, the man I once loved and would do anything for became the man I hated the most. The man I would do anything to not be seen with. That's how drastically the relationship dynamic between me and my father changed. For me, family is everything; it isn't a phrase I was taught but something I witnessed. I initially believed it because as a child, I saw everything to make me believe the family was everything. Unfortunately, once the abuse started, I had every reason to believe the opposite. All of that wasn't as easy as I'm saying now. For a long time, I battled the idea of whether my father was still everything despite the abuse. Should my father still mean the world to me even if he was the root of my pain?

I couldn't shake the feeling that I had to tell someone about the abuse one day. But I hesitated, thinking about what would happen if I did. I felt guilty—if I exposed him, it would ruin his reputation. Then I started feeling sorry for him. I pictured others turning their backs on him once they found out what he'd been up to in secret. But one day, I knew I had to speak up to save myself.

A few more years later, I finally decided to break my silence. To start my journey to be free from the trauma. I wanted to find out who I was beyond the abuse and its emotional baggage. I was desperate to know the girl I wasn't. That journey for me began when I learned my family wasn't everything, despite what I had been taught.

It started when I realised that my emotions towards my father were valid. So, I didn't need to feel guilty for the spiral of emotions I had towards him and the abuse. But it was just as important to realise that as much as I felt deep hatred, I didn't want to carry it with me forever. Even though it's been a couple of years since I broke my silence, it's only recently that I've come to accept that family doesn't have to be everything if it's not.

Coming to this realisation wasn't easy. I had long periods of hoping that one day, my family would change. I was hurt that my loved ones could treat me so badly. But I stayed, hoping one day they'd realise the pain they caused and apologise. This did nothing but leave me more hurt because that point never came. I never wanted to leave my family, but each day, they gave me reasons to. When I needed them most, they showed me they didn't care about my pain until I got to the point of being forced to let go. Letting go wasn't easy, as I found myself in a cycle of leaving and then coming back. I was leaving for the wrong reasons. I was leaving so they could feel the pain of losing me; I wasn't leaving because I knew I deserved better.

I found the courage to move on. But I often felt lonely. This made me question if my family was really that bad or if i should tolerate them and go back. There were times when I wanted to go back and firm the pain because I couldn't bear the loneliness. But I had to remind myself that it hurts to leave the family I once loved so much. But the pain of leaving is nothing compared to the pain of staying. It goes without saying that the betrayal of being hurt by the people you trust most runs deep. Letting go isn't something I chose to do but rather something I was forced to do. I had to get a lot thrown in my face before I could decide to move away, and it was only then I was able to heal.

**Family is everything**

Family is something which nobody can take away from you. It's something that's with you from birth until you die. That being said, your family is supposed to be your safe place. The place where you know that whatever you go through, there will always be a group of people ready to support you. A family is supposed to be a ride-or-die type of relationship. With human flaws, you find that sometimes family isn't any of these things. It's important to know that family can only be everything if they show you they are everything. Actions will always speak louder than words. Suppose your family runs on the theme that nobody comes before family, and they are everything. In that case, their actions must also back that up. Family can mean a lot to many people, but it's also okay to accept your family as toxic, even if you have been taught that family is everything no matter what. It's good to draw a line with your family when they go too far. Don't feel pressured to see them as perfect despite their behaviour. Assuming everyone respects those boundaries, people can maintain a healthy relationship this way. Choosing a boundary and sticking to it shows your growth. You are learning your worth and what you can't tolerate, even from close people.

Believing family is everything, even in the presence of abuse, then your idea of family becomes flawed. The idea that family should mean everything to you, no matter how imperfect they are, actually takes away from what a healthy family is. It infects other areas of your life, leading you to settle for less while believing it is enough. For example, staying in a relationship despite the other person constantly hurting you.

**Love your parents no matter what**

The expectation to love your parents no matter what encourages staying close to caregivers despite them hurting you. From a young age, most people learn that family is the highest form of relationship they will ever have. You are expected to let someone off if they have a family title. This means if they do something, they should be let off because of the relationship you are supposed to have with them.

Other family members often let them off too. They believe that, with family, situations can be brushed under the carpet even with knowing what the other family member did isn't okay. So, for example, in my case, my biological father was the abuser. My other relatives let him off because it was a father-daughter relationship. To them, it didn't look as bad because we were supposed to have a close biological relationship. Phrases like, "At the end of the day, that's your dad," don't only dismiss the victim but also side with the abuser.

If the abuser is let off because of their relationship with you, the same energy should apply to hold them accountable because of your relationship with them. Read that again. So, my father should have been held more accountable because we are closely related. Instead, he was let off because, at the end of the day, he was my 'dad'. What isn't acceptable from a stranger shouldn't be accepted from a family member either. Strangers don't owe us anything, but family do. Take care of yourself when your family disregards your feelings. Make choices that help you even if they don't get it. Your mental health is top a priority.

Doing what's best for you may mean leaving the current environment that you're in most times. While your family showed that family isn't everything, there are still families out there who prove the opposite. Giving you hope that you can also build a family that truly reflects what everything is.

**Your parents and their parents**

Maybe your family was dismissive. They may have invalidated your feelings. Or, they may have even blamed you for the situation. Whatever the response, it's essential to acknowledge its impact on your healing process. By doing so, you can know how it has affected your emotional state.

Your parents' behaviours in family life are a reflection of how their own parents acted in a family setting. Generational patterns can stick around for a while. Parents who were expected to stay in their family no matter what are likely to expect the same from you. The same expectation is imposed on you, continuing this generational cycle. They will expect you to keep in touch with the abuser. That's what they did or saw their parents do. That said, it's almost too simple to find yourself stuck in this generational cycle of staying no matter what someone does to you. Remember, abuse is likely not a one-time thing in your family. It's been happening for decades, but no one did anything. They dismissed it because, to them, blood is thicker than water. This generational cycle ends with you. There are limits to what can be tolerated, and abuse has gone way above the line. It may have started with them, but it will definitely end with you.

The rest of the family either ignores it or is hypocritical. They preach one thing but do the opposite. Even after trauma, if the family situation is fixable, then it's worth working together to mend the fractured relationships. If your concerns are still overlooked and their actions are inconsistent, it may be time to step back. Consider if this environment is the right fit for you. There will be places where you will truly thrive, and that doesn't have to be in your family setting.

Family can be the root cause of the trauma you have to heal from. When the people closest to you become toxic, you are left with no choice but to cut them loose, especially when they are the source of your pain. Sometimes, you need space from the ones who hurt you to heal. Find your own way to peace, even if it takes you somewhere new. It's tough, but you'd do yourself a big favour by distancing and choosing yourself. The wound that still bleeds due to their dismissiveness will never stop bleeding until you leave. It's better to be without a family than to stay in a toxic one. You need to realise that healing for you won't just be healing from the cut the abuser made. You are also healing from your family's responses, which cut that wound deeper. Healing from the views of the individuals who were meant to support your healing. So remember not to excuse the abuse just because they are family. Not all family ties are healthy. You deserve positive and supportive connections. You have the power to choose relationships that lift you up. Surround yourself with people who aren't detrimental to your well-being.

**Is my family still everything?**

If you can fix the family conflict, please do it. Work to mend those broken relationships. Always remember that some people really do love you, and others you will meet will truly care for you. So even if you don't get to choose family, you do get to make friends with people who end up becoming family.

Being around those who care for you is always healing. Building on new relationships can help you fill the void that you may have when you are no longer in contact with the people you love but can't stay with. The phrase "family is everything" isn't inherited. It's earned through action. If family members act without remorse, they prove that family isn't everything. Allow yourself to be free from feeling guilty of choosing yourself and leaving. It's better to start from scratch than to continue building on a collapsing environment. Choosing you doesn't make you a bad person. Sometimes, it's hard to choose you when you've spent your whole life choosing everyone else. Choose you today. So you don't spend a lifetime choosing people who choose themselves.

**A toxic family won't come from you.**

If you come from a toxic family, accept that you didn't create it. With that being said, you don't need to be a part of it either. You're free to step back from relationships that hurt you. Don't feel like you owe it to anyone to stay stuck in toxic patterns. You have the power to make your own way without carrying others' baggage. Pick peace over duty. Sometimes, you feel wrong or guilty about doing the right thing. Ditching a toxic home life you didn't ask for is key to finding yourself again. For a long time, not getting what you needed as a kid leaves you feeling guilty when you choose yourself for the first time. It's hard to choose you, especially since everyone gave you a reason not to. But it's necessary for you to overcome the trauma that the abuser caused. People won't like the boundaries you set because they can't use you like they used to. Your family dysfunction existed long before you were born. It's unfortunate you got caught in their unresolved issues.

Family should be more than a title. Being family doesn't exempt them from certain things. People who share your DNA do not automatically deserve a connection with you. Exempting family from accountability downplays the hurt they have caused. This isn't about being unforgiving but about acknowledging the pain they've inflicted. Letting family off says their actions had no real consequences. Your growth and healing are more important. If your family is restricting or enabling things that hinder your progress, that's not what one expects of family.

Sometimes, the fear of being hurt or mistreated can cause you to act selfishly. You become too harsh on other family members connected to the abuser. Even when they don't have a part to play in your pain, you still manage to find something to mark them down on.

# It's not what they did

When the abuser was your primary caregiver, the process of healing from their trauma is not just about what they did. It's equally about the responsibilities they neglected. Caregivers are entrusted with the task of nurturing the child. However, in some cases, the child who should be the one receiving care, ends up providing it instead. The typical dynamic where the parent cares for the child, is inverted, forcing the child into a parental role.

Unresolved childhood trauma can hold parents back emotionally. If they don't heal their inner wounds, they can get stuck mentally at the age when the trauma started. Those wounds were carried into parenthood. Their own baggage got in the way of giving you the love and care you needed when you were growing up. The worst thing is you have to face the consequences of what your parents never dealt with.

It's okay to feel empathy for the challenges caregivers faced in the past. But those struggles don't excuse any toxic behaviours they have. As much as hurt people do hurt people, they also have a choice to not hurt people. You can be a product of your past but, you don't need to be chained to it. So, even though your past has shaped you to be who you are right now, it doesn't mean you need to be that person forever. Since caregivers didn't address their trauma, they stayed emotionally immature. You had to deal with parents who had a childlike mentality. Your childhood faded and was replaced with the burden of being a parent to those who were supposed to parent you. That heavy burden was never meant for small shoulders to bear. Unfortunately, you matured too quickly, taking on heavy responsibilities before your time. This maturity is mistaken for having a good upbringing.

**Acceptance of needs not met**

The people who took care of you while growing up were supposed to be the main guides in your life. They had the responsibility of raising you in a way they would want you to grow up. It goes without saying they also needed to meet your needs and provide a safe environment for you to grow up in. Unfortunately, not everyone got this type of support from their caregivers. Many found themselves in abusive homes. Their caregivers neglected them and denied their basic needs. Childhood emotional neglect doesn't erase needs. Your first point of contact being cut off didn't take away from the fact your emotional needs still needed to be met. You needed a substitute to meet them. To a hungry soul every bitter thing is sweet. The void of unmet needs now keeps you going for things which aren't good for you all for the sake of being filled up.

This is now where you, as a child, were forced to meet your own needs. Just like a child who had to parent their parents, it's impossible for a child to meet their own emotional needs. So, you ended up neglected instead. Meeting your own needs was a responsibility too hard to fulfil. You accepted that your needs would never be met. With no one to look after you, you became very independent at a young age. Your emotions either had to be suppressed or controlled in a toxic and damaging way. It goes without saying that anything suppressed or ignored starts to make a sound sooner or later. The consequences of extreme child independence are paid for in adulthood.

## The parental role in relationships

The parent role which you had to fulfil as a child naturally becomes a part of you when you are older. And because the parent role becomes a part of who you are, there's always going to be a need to satisfy it. Without intent, you are drawn to friendships and relationships that allow you to be the parent. A relationship that offers this will make you feel like you belong. Any relationships you form need to have space for you to display the parent in you; otherwise, it wouldn't work. Friendships or relationships which don't allow you to be the parent younger you always was, will make you feel unsettled. You will think the relationship isn't working out, only because they don't give you something that soothes that wounded part of you.

Using the same behaviours in each new relationship creates a pattern. You get the same response or outcome each time. This isn't a coincidence. Your relationships' outcomes come from patterns you've developed over time. By recognising these patterns, you can begin to break them. Each new relationship is an opportunity for growth and change.

With self-awareness and a willingness to heal, you can build stronger, more meaningful connections

Now, for friendships. You unknowingly build them with people you can show up for more than they show up for themselves. This means befriending people who are broken as much or more than you are. That way, you can fill the void you have and compensate for this parent role. By doing so, you become an emotional parent to them, providing support much like a parent would. Having these types of friendships requires you to do more for them than they will ever be able to do for you. This will be easy for you if you are the type of friend who will give up everything to make sure your friends are okay. But it will end up leaving you drained and exhausted. You can't pour from an empty cup, let alone from a broken cup. After all you've been through, you'll want someone to be there for you. But if that's not available, you'll be drained trying to support others who are just as bruised as you.

After all you have been through, it's easy to believe that no one will ever go out of their way for you as you do for them. This may feel true if your past left you feeling unappreciated and overlooked. You've learned to put others first. You fulfil their needs while sacrificing your own desires. You go above and beyond to meet the needs of others because that's something you wish you could do for yourself. Remember that what happened in the past and how it made you feel doesn't have to spill into your future. Being let down doesn't take away from the fact that you will find people who will go above and beyond for you.

Everyone wants to feel love at least once in their lives, if not their whole life. It goes without saying that the parent role can have a huge effect on your love life. You may find yourself stuck in a cycle of always going for partners whom you have to baby and be responsible for. This cycle can show up in different ways. For example, dating partners who are emotionally immature or too dependent on you. You end up in this cycle where you treat your partner like a child. A relationship needs to have balance. When you treat your partner like your son, you find you are giving almost all the emotional support, if not all. But they appear to be incapable of doing the same for you. This serves as evidence you still have the parent role ingrained. You seek to satisfy it through the partners you choose.

## Love that's far-fetched

Growing up, having to meet your needs forces you to be self-sufficient from a young age. As an adult, the idea of receiving love and care from others feels far-fetched and hard to find. Living in a house where you had to earn love makes you believe you always need to do something to be loved. When someone loves you without you doing anything, it feels wrong. You may not know how to accept or return affection, making it hard for you to form and keep close relationships. Having to take care of yourself from a young age can make it feel like love is a luxury. It is something you can't access rather than something everyone needs.

You will meet someone who likes you without you having to do anything. You will feel stupid because of how easy the love is. You are used to working for your love. But, you will question yourself when you can't trace back what you did for that person to like you. This can feel strange when you are used to working hard to earn someone's love. You will feel stupid because of how easy it is. This is a gentle reminder that not every situation will be like your childhood.

People like you for you; you are a great person to be around. So they don't like you because of anything you did. They like you because you are you.

**Pauline's story: Hard to accept I was denied something**

I knew my father's actions were hurting me. But, when I did something small that upset him, it made 15-year-old me upset. I considered his feelings over mine. How he felt was all that mattered, so as long as he was fine, I was fine. To be quite frank, I didn't care about myself as much. On one occasion, I ran away from home. I was going through a lot mentally, but I still couldn't put 2 and 2 together to figure out why I was reacting the way I was. Despite the abuse, I still couldn't connect the dots. I didn't think it was the abuse that was affecting my behaviour. Back to the story, before sneaking out, I made sure it was dark and that nobody was aware of my whereabouts. I didn't want anyone to know. If they did, I'd get in trouble. I also wanted to stress them out. I wanted them to feel the stress of searching for me. I successfully managed to sneak out, and more than a couple hours later, I got home safely.

To no surprise, when I entered the house, my father immediately started complaining. He went on a tangent about how everything I was doing made him unhappy and stressed. When I thought he was finished, he went off to angrily mention that he'd rather me dead for his own peace. Those words stuck with me and made me have this immense guilt lingering in my head. Extreme sadness hovered over me like a dark cloud I couldn't take away. I felt sorrowful that my actions were affecting him this much. A conversation that should have hurt me made me feel guilty instead. I didn't deserve to be told any of that. But, even with that, I blamed myself. I convinced myself I should have been a better child so I wouldn't hurt my father's feelings.

I felt like such a bad person because I had yet once again hurt my father's feelings. Over the weeks, I started hating myself for not being able to control my actions. At that age, I was tricked into believing my father was my best friend. So, knowing I caused his stress and unhappiness really hurt me.

Now that I'm older, I understand why I was the way I was. And why I still cared for my father despite the pain and hurt he was causing me. Reflecting back, I can tell you that the relationship I had with my father was one in which I was his parent. I felt like I was in charge of his emotions, so when he was upset, I would feel extremely disappointed in myself. My actions towards him would eat me up and keep me up at night. My father looked innocent because I viewed him as a child, so his wrongs were overlooked. When the abuse started, I became a parent to my father. This was a dangerous thing for me. When he hurt me, I made excuses for him and gave him the benefit of the doubt. In my mind, I saw him as someone younger than me. I felt I needed to protect him at all costs. I treated him like he meant everything and more, but he couldn't even do the bare minimum for me. I always pushed aside the abuse. Despite his hurtful actions, I had a strong urge to be the bigger person. I saw his actions as accidents and as nothing that was intentional. My parental nature made me protective of my father. So, it was hard to accept that I was denied something. Becoming parents to your parents makes it harder to accept their behaviour was wrong and abusive. Even in cases where you know the behaviour is wrong, you may have excused them and given them leeway. Convincing yourself that the person hurting you doesn't know it lessens the pain. You now see it as accidental, not intentional.

Being at such a young age probably means you didn't understand when you were being mistreated by the people you trust. But if you did get it, there would have been a big change in your behaviour. Your actions towards your caregivers would have changed to reflect how they were treating you. You would have been a lot more angry and resentful towards them. The unawareness kept you seeking love from those who hurt you the most. Your love and protectiveness for them only came from one thing. You hadn't yet understood the life-changing effects of having an abusive caregiver.

# THE PREDATOR AND TRAUMA

# The Predator

Strangers don't owe you any loyalty but your family do. When the abuse comes from someone you trust, healing from it is more than just healing from the trauma. You are also healing from the betrayal of being hurt by the person who was supposed to protect you. This type of betrayal makes it difficult to trust again.

Betrayal cuts deep, but healing begins when you face the pain. Healing from betrayal means acknowledging the pain it caused. It's also important to remember that not everyone is out there to betray your trust. Being vulnerable and opening up will be hard, but it will help you restore your faith in humanity.

**But at the end of the day, that's your...**

I remember a few years back, I opened up to a lady about my life and the abuse I had faced. She asked who did it and whether it was someone she knew. I told her my father was the abuser. She looked shocked and did not know what to say. After a while, she continued the conversation by telling me, 'But at the end of the day, that's your dad.'

Family ties aren't magic erasers for the pain. Being related doesn't take away from the wounds they created. What matters is what they did, not how they are related to you. They will expect you to forgive and act like nothing happened just because it's family. You can't shake off the memory of what happened. There's a conflict between the relationship with the abuser and the abuse itself. Leaving you stuck trying to make sense of how you should feel about the person who was to care for you being the one who hurt you instead. You start to wonder if what really happened was even that bad. You question whether the person who hurt you should be excused because they are a family member. The close connection you were supposed to have doesn't hide them from the truth of what they did.

The phrase in itself is dismissive of what happened, and what it does is put more focus on the relationship the abuser has with you rather than what they did. You're expected to see and love the perpetrator the same because they are your family or caregivers. Those who make this ignorant statement fail to understand that a child abused by a caregiver is never the same. The effects of going through abuse are so big, and they alter someone's life completely. People also fail to understand that the fact that a parent or family member is the abuser is why it hurts so much more. Strangers don't owe you anything, but your caregivers do.

When family members do something wrong, it is usually excused, hidden and not talked about because it's family. The family runs on the dysfunction of its unresolved issues. They bond with each other over dysfunctions that have never been dealt with. So, the abuser sometimes isn't held accountable. Abuse is often seen as normal. It's all swept away. Remember, just because the abuse was from a family member doesn't make it less of a big deal. Blood doesn't change the severity of any situation. If it wouldn't be okay if a stranger did it to you, then it shouldn't be nearly okay if a family member did it.

## Regaining the relationship with the predator

It's completely normal to want things to go back to the way they used to be before the abuse started. This isn't always possible, especially when the abuser is unremorseful of the harm they caused you. Boundaries must be set in place to make sure you don't face any further pain from the perpetrators even after the abuse has stopped. It is clear that, in some cases, the predator will admit their selfish desires caused harm. They will then work to rebuild the broken relationship. But, even with the rekindled relationship, nothing is the same. It takes much trust and bravery to fully rebuild it. This isn't the case for everyone. Some abusers refuse to be accountable for their actions. They aren't willing to acknowledge that their actions hurt someone. Their character reveals a lot about who they are, so there is no point in rekindling a relationship with these types of predators.

## The predator

Hurt people do sometimes hurt others. That may be the case for some perpetrators who themselves would have gone through abuse. If they never dealt with their trauma, they will never realise how much it cost them. Not healing from it makes it easier to hurt someone else the same way. Knowing the cost and pain you endured can stop you from hurting someone else. You can't bear to put anyone through what you went through. It would be selfish to do so. You know the price and wouldn't want someone else to pay it.

Perpetrators always disguise themselves as good people. The perpetrator would normally be nice and act like they care and truly love the victim. From an outsider's point of view, nothing is wrong. This facade is put up so that people don't suspect them. If they get accused, it makes it hard to believe the victim. People won't believe this "nice person" could do such a bad thing. It is easy to trust people who seem nice and genuine. Many perpetrators hide their true intentions behind a good appearance. It helps them avoid suspicion. By doing so, they deceive their victims and make it hard for others to believe the claims of those who suffered abuse.

## Care and love for the victim

Manipulation from the person hurting you keeps you loving them and hating yourself. It's what starts and keeps the abuse going. Predators make their victims rely on them by acting kind and helpful. They create a false sense of trust. When the predator is close in care they will often use fake nurturing techniques. They are used to build a closer relationship with the child. They will do everything in their power so the victim trusts them. They pretend to be the most loving person. But really, they seek control by manipulating the child's perception of them. This looks like love-bombing and grooming the child with gifts and words of affirmation to hide their bad intentions. Then, once they have done that, they use it to their advantage. They create this special bond that looks amazing to outsiders. When victims finally speak up, people often doubt them. The abuser's fake public image makes their bad deeds seem impossible to believe. To make matters worse, the child may feel guilty due to a bond with the abuser. Victims often struggle to report abuse, feeling that they're betraying the one who hurt them. It may prevent them from doing things that could help, like reporting the abuse. Sadly, those who faced abuse often feel guilty when trying to help themselves. In the child's mind, they love them. So, guilt eats at them. They fear that opening up might hurt the predator's feelings. This emotional trap silences many and keeps them in a cycle of self-blame.

**Pauline's story**

My biological father used tactics to gain my trust whilst also instilling fear. He would take me to nice places and make sure he did what he didn't do for others so I could feel special and extra loved. He made me completely depend on him despite having others around me whom I could have also depended on. After some time, it got to a point where I couldn't go to anyone else except for my father for help. So, even when he was hurting me, I had to go to him. Younger me believed that my father's acts were genuine and that he was slightly flawed. Little did I know that all the love, care, and gifts were all for a specific purpose. It was all a plan to make sure that he could silence me for many years. Unpacking my past and everything I had been through hurt. It hurt more to know that even the happy memories I had from my childhood had hidden agendas.

The predators may have masked themselves to look good. After a while, they took it off, revealing the beast behind it. This is why it's so hard to break the silence. To others, the predator is an amazing superhero. But to you, he's the opposite. It makes it harder because people are quick to deny it. They say the person who hurt you couldn't have been the one who hurt you. But, this is a common tactic of most predators, especially with child victims.

**Pauline's story: Grieving what you never had**

After abuse, people assume you hate the abuser and want no ties to them. If you had a good relationship before the abuse, a part of you could still love them while grieving the relationship which died long ago.

When I was younger, I saw my father as the best thing to ever exist, except for the abuse he was inflicting on me. I always wished he wasn't doing what he was doing because then that would have made him the perfect father for me. Before I learnt who my father was behind that mask, I always yearned to be close to him. I saw him as the fantasy version of the father I wanted instead of seeing him as the father he was.

As a child, I used what I saw. If someone did one bad thing, I'd think they were good, even if the bad thing was really bad. It was just one bad thing, so the flaw's size didn't matter. As I got older, I could see and understand more. I realised my idea of my father being a good person was a fantasy based on what he was showing me. He had many hidden layers that had yet to be revealed. I realised my father only seemed good because of the power he had. He got everything his way, so of course, he would be good. Growing up for me was realising that the abuse wasn't just one bad thing a perfect man was doing. It became clearer by day that my father was a lot more toxic than I ever could have believed him to be. The abuse being the "only bad thing about him" meant there must be more wrong with him that had yet to be exposed.

When his toxic traits and narcissism were exposed, I began to have conflicting feelings towards him. I was shocked by the way he portrayed himself and who he played himself to be.

**Conflicting feelings about the abuser**

It's hard to navigate conflicting feelings about an abusive family member. To avoid conflicting feelings, look at what happened from the outside perspective. It's easy to lose perspective when you are the one who went through the experience. Imagine if what happened to you happened to someone you are close to and care about. This lets you see the situation's severity. If it happened to someone else, you'd be angry at the abuser's actions.

After enduring something for so long, you become numb to the pain. But, as you heal, your pain tolerance will drop. This will let you be kinder to yourself. You'll see that it really did hurt to go through what they put you through. Realising the pain they caused will show you how deep it is. Whether a family member or a stranger, it doesn't matter who did it. It is still unacceptable. True family is not just about who you're related to, but how they act towards you. Those who treat you like family prove their loyalty and commitment through their actions. If someone doesn't live up to what it means to be a good family member, then they don't deserve to be considered one, no matter how they're connected. It's okay to let go of toxic families the same way it's okay to let go of toxic friendships and relationships. Validating your feelings will help you see through your abuser's brainwashing. It will show you the extent of the abuse you faced. You have to choose yourself; it will hurt at first, but you will thank yourself later. You did nothing to deserve what happened to you. You are not responsible for how they treated you, so you don't owe them anything. You deserve freedom from the torment they put you through. Your family's refusal to see your pain no longer defines you. You're not just better off without them. You're destined for greatness beyond their limitations. Face your pain, then leave it in the dust. Your path to freedom starts today.

**Holding the perpetrator accountable**

Making someone own up to their actions is draining and exhausting. Especially when they purposely refuse to acknowledge their wrongdoings. Holding the predator accountable won't undo the harm. The damage from what they did still lingers. The survivors' feelings are valid. Their suffering matters, regardless of whether the predator admits to it. Helping the survivors heal and recover from their trauma is the priority. More damage can come from trying to hold the abuser accountable. They will deny the allegations. They'll even accuse the survivors of lying.

**Overcoming betrayal**

Healing from betrayal takes bravery and the willingness to be slightly hurt again. Each step you take might remind you of past hurts. But by confronting that pain, you can learn to rebuild the broken trust. The goal is to get to the point where you can trust people again without living life based on the pain of the last person who hurt you. The hurt from the past doesn't have to control your life forever.

As you process the betrayal, know that what they did has nothing to do with you; rather, it says more about them. Those who are cruel never care how their actions might affect someone. When someone is selfish, you'll see it in how they treat others. What they do speaks volumes about who they are. The betrayal is a reflection of their character, not your misjudgement. Good people do exist, though it's hard to believe. The fact that you are a good person and you exist is why you should have hope that there's more out there like you. Not everyone is out there to hurt you. Some people really do love you, and others you will meet will genuinely love you.

Regaining trust is hard, especially when betrayal is a huge part of your childhood. You need to process the betrayal; don't brush it under the carpet. Also, be aware that someone betraying you doesn't mean you shouldn't trust other people. I know people have let you down, but remember, not everyone is like the person who hurt you. Everyone is different, and everyone has a different character. So why would the same concept for the person who hurt you apply to everyone else if they are different?

**How do you regain trust after betrayal?**

Learning how to trust again means seeing the good in others, even if you are inclined to see the bad. Take the risk of building genuine relationships without insecurities being at the centre. As for any experience, it's important to talk about the betrayal. You don't have to talk to the person who hurt you. But open up to someone else. Discuss what happened and how it affected you. Talking helps you notice how the betrayals have affected your life and relationships.

What you don't realise is that betrayal makes you super alert. It leaves you constantly looking for a sign that someone will hurt you. To avoid getting hurt again, you might start pushing people away. It's a defence mechanism to prevent future pain. Sometimes, you can feel like others are out there to hurt you, leading you to search for signs to confirm that worry. If you don't address this, you might distance yourself from genuine people. Noticing these patterns means you can learn and heal from the past to live a life that isn't run by it. It takes time, but it does happen.

Such experiences can create deep trust issues. It's important to know that not everyone is like the person who hurt you. It's hard to see life positively when all you have had are bad experiences. It's hard to see the good in people, especially when your closest people cut you the deepest. Don't feel pressured to trust people to prove you're learning. The process of learning to trust again needs boundaries. Trust is earned. If someone isn't proving they can be trusted, don't force yourself to trust them.

# Speaking to a brick wall

Childhood trauma survivors often confront their abusers, expressing the pain they've endured. This is a big step which is supposed to give them a chance to have closure by talking directly to them. Most of the time, the predator doesn't care about what they did or the harm it caused. For the victim, it always ends up like they are speaking to a brick wall. Speaking to a brick wall means trying to speak to someone but when you do, your words fall flat on a wall. They dismiss you either by being silent or changing the topic. If the person does respond they often miss the whole point you are trying to get to them entirely. Some words go in one ear and out the other. They only choose to hear what they want. Anything which doesn't suit them gets tuned out. No matter how hard you try, your emotions never reach them. Words just can't capture it. Your emotions go so much deeper. It's frustrating when nobody is trying to hear you out. There's this slight hope about the broken relationship with this person, which is why you keep trying to get them to hear you. You assume they will hear you and understand how their actions hurt you. But when they don't and instead show no concern for how you're feeling, that adds insult to the injury. You're hurt twice - once by what they did, and again by their lack of care. Each time they don't respond, your hope for the relationship fades. Every expression gets no reply. You can't get through to them, leaving you exhausted. Eventually, you stop expressing your feelings to both the person who hurt you and to others in the future.

**Fear of not being understood**

It goes without saying everything that happens in your childhood directly impacts your adulthood. Repeating yourself and not being understood will make you fear opening up. You will know you have reached this point when conversations start to fade away right in the middle. Things are left unsaid. Your mind starts racing, making connections, and figuring people won't understand you. You start making assumptions: they probably won't get it anyway.

You'll sense this shift subtly. Conversations trail off mid-sentence. Thoughts remain unspoken. To remove the burden of not being understood, you just need to stop talking.

Without knowing it, you find you have reached the point where you don't want to waste your breath to then not be heard. The opposite can happen, where you over explain yourself. When you spoke when you were younger, you weren't heard, and you had to say the same thing again and again. Now you feel like you have to repeat the same thing again and again in order to be understood.

**Am I saying the right thing?**

Before the abuse stopped, there were so many times I attempted to speak to my father about what he was doing to me. Getting an apology from him was all I wanted. I figured I could continue loving him if he apologised. It would have shown my younger self that, despite what he did, he was sorry about it. I was naive, so I believed an apology would show that he still cared about me.

Despite repeatedly expressing the same things to my father, I never received an apology at all. Rather, I was always dismissed with silence. I was manipulated daily to the point I saw myself as the problem. Now, thinking back to it, all that little girl wanted was to be loved by her father. She wanted to be shown that he cared about her.

After the constant manipulation, I started hating myself because I couldn't hate him. In my eyes, he was flawless despite what he was doing. It's only through maturity that I have learnt that a loving father won't hurt you on purpose, knowing they are hurting you.

Being a child, I found it hard to see my father's flaws. What he was doing to me was the only flaw I saw in him. To younger me that wasn't much because it was just 1 flaw and everything else was fine. I thought if we could get past what he was doing to me, then everything would have been great. Now that I'm older and not naive anymore, I've come to realise that it isn't that easy. Being dismissed by the person who abused me cut deeper than i thought. I repeatedly voiced my pain only to face more hurt.

It's frustrating talking to someone and they don't seem to understand you. It gets to a point where you start to question if you are using the right words. It can leave you wondering if they are just choosing not to understand you. And most of the time, it's not like they don't actually understand you but have chosen not to. Think about it, what person is told the same story in different ways but doesn't capture anything from that story? It's like sending a long message to a partner about what they did, and they reply to you with, "What do you mean?" Sometimes, it's a case of using the wrong words. But, when a child tries to tell an adult about something the adult is doing or did to them, the adult simply ignores. They prefer to show the child that they don't care. They decide to show the child that their feelings aren't valid to them. These types of people will always dismiss your feelings and make the subject about them. Everything you say to them, they will always manage to make that scenario about them. They will make themselves the victim and make you the villain. According to them, everything you say is an attack. Trying to explain yourself to this person will hurt you more. All they will keep doing is dismissing you.

A person won't hurt you from a place of love knowing they have hurt you. The person you are trying to make understand is someone who hurt you before. Most of the time, this person is someone you are close to, which is why it hurts when they act like a brick wall. You need to move on when you notice that the person doesn't show interest in or value your thoughts and feelings. If you mean something to them, they will show you that you do matter to them. Continue working on yourself because nobody loves you unless you love yourself. Learn to value yourself without outside validation. That way, you can spend time with people who also value you instead of trying to force those who don't value you to see the value in you.

**How repeating yourself is affecting you**

Low self-esteem comes out from situations like these. Explaining the same thing again and again and not being understood will have you doubting if anyone is ever going to get what's going on inside you. The struggle to be understood is draining, and it's like words just aren't enough. It's almost like if a grown person couldn't understand you as a child, why would anyone understand you now? This is where most of the damage starts because you start to hide away more, and you start being silent. It's not even like you don't want to say how you are feeling, but the thought of having to re-explain your feelings is exhausting. You don't want to feel the pressure of saying it twice and still being misunderstood.

I noticed there was a big difference in how the younger me responded to speaking to a brick wall versus when I got older. When the younger me wasn't understood, she started rebelling. She had this idea that if my father couldn't understand what I was saying to him, then he shouldn't expect me to understand or do anything he said. It was a rebellion, so he could feel what it felt like to speak to someone who didn't listen. All those years of not being heard accumulated pain. As I got older, it was hard to let out my feelings because I had been accumulating for so long. I'd been conditioned to believe I won't be understood. Every attempt to express what was hidden deep inside always led me to feel this physical exhaustion.

If what is felt can't be expressed in a healthy way, it will definitely be expressed in one way or another. So, as I got older, the relationship with my father got worse because I was becoming more aware that I had been violated. I was becoming more aware of other things which he had done and how severely they had affected me. Even though my words couldn't express how I truly felt, my body showed the hidden pain through anger. My anger towards my father was a sign that I was finally aware of how severe the impact of the abuse was. It was a way of showing my pain towards the one who caused it.

### Stop talking

It is a hard pill to swallow, but if swallowed earlier, you can dodge the effects of certain situations. It would remove the exhaustion you feel when you speak. There are days where you may have felt like you were the issue. Here is a gentle reminder that it was never you. Knowing this lifts a weight off your shoulders. It makes it easier to stop explaining the same thing to them. Despite this, you shouldn't keep quiet; rather, find one person to speak to about it.

Jeremiah 17:23 mentions ancestors who were like speaking to a brick wall. They were told not to work on the Sabbath. But, they "made their neck stiff" and wouldn't listen. The thing about these ancestors is that they didn't listen, and they weren't trying to either. They didn't make an effort to listen. This is the exact same for many abusers. Not only do they not hear the words of the victims, but they harden themselves to not understand too.

You shouldn't dismiss speaking out to the perpetrator entirely. You should make it your priority not to dwell on explaining to the perpetrator. At the end of the day, if they were okay with hurting you, they wouldn't understand why it's hurting you in the first place. Once you realise that someone always dismisses your feelings, you need to withdraw. Protect your heart by staying neutral. When your feelings are ignored, create some space. Take care of yourself by stepping back and letting go. Healthy emotional detachment protects you from those who disregard your feelings.

Don't invest your emotions. When someone refuses to listen to you it also means genuine apologies and empathy are off the table. Expressing yourself more won't make them understand unless they choose to. For your own peace you need to let it. No more trying to get them to listen let alone begging them to see your pain. Continuing to seek validation means they have you where they want you.

**Your feelings are still valid despite not being heard.**

Someone not hearing you out when you are trying to tell them how you are feeling doesn't mean that your feelings aren't valid. It just means they don't want to listen to you.

Know that being dismissed doesn't make your feelings any less real. It'll be easier to let go of the disappointment that comes with people not listening. What you say will fall on deaf ears, but doesn't take away from how you feel. It will be easier to shake off your disappointment when no interest is shown. This takes a high level of maturity.

When you are alone is what matters, the satisfaction you feel inside without any outward influence is what matters. You live with yourself daily. So, you must be satisfied with yourself. The outside world doesn't matter if you don't have true satisfaction. Without it, you will be searching for something you will never find because it starts from the inside. The whole world could think you are beautiful, for example, but that won't matter to you until you see yourself as that.

Being told your pain isn't bad enough can be damaging. It can make you doubt your feelings and make you question if it's that deep in the first place. Whoever tells you this doesn't even have the right to. Unless someone has lived your life, they won't understand how deeply your past affects you. No one will ever be able to understand the places you have had to dig yourself up from, and because of that, they can never have a say in how you feel. The way you feel is valid because what you went through changed everything about you. No one will realise that because they aren't you and they didn't go through what you did. Saying someone can't be sad because others have it worse is like saying they can't be happy because someone has it better.

### Seeking approval from those who hurt you

What you don't realise is that when your caregivers hurt you as a child, you don't begin to hate them for hurting you. You start to hate yourself for what is happening to you. That's the only way you survived the trauma because you hated yourself and not them. When you get older, it's hard to break through this love-and-hate relationship you have towards your caregivers. This means you may still seek your caregivers' love as an adult. You may have come to terms that they aren't good for you but you still want their approval.

If they never validated your feelings when you were younger, they won't validate them now. But there's this slight hope that they will validate them now even though it's clear that they aren't going to do it. Moving on from this takes a lot of self-love. You have to get to a point where you decide that nothing is worth the disappointment you get when you try to seek approval from your parents.

As you continue to practice self-love and find good people to surround yourself with, you will find this becomes a lot easier. Also, remember, if you aren't able to trust someone you have a relationship with, then the relationship has no foundation.

# No Violence

After many years of pushing my pain under the carpet, I temporarily forgot what I had been through. I still believe that's the only way I was able to survive the abuse all through.

It was a sunny, golden hour day, 3 years after the abuse had stopped. I was in my room when it all came back to me.

'You were abused…'

'You were abused by your dad for all these years...'

'Wait a minute, no way, I have faced abuse all this time.'

'He really took advantage of me; there's no way; how did I forget all of that.'

'Omg, you really did get abused. What the hell!'

That's what my thoughts for those 30 minutes were like. I went back and forth with myself, shocked at my reality over the last few years. I couldn't understand how I had forgotten it all this time, and now it was coming back to me on a random day. I wasn't doing or thinking of anything that would have triggered the memories. They appeared out of nowhere.

I knew I wasn't making it up, but at certain points, it felt like I was. It was hard to comprehend that my memory wasn't just a story but, in fact, my reality for six years of my childhood. As much as I had come to have knowledge that I had been abused, I still doubted myself. What I went through was horrible, yet I couldn't get myself to believe that. I knew I had been abused. I felt so dramatic, even claiming it was abuse. The more I wanted to come into agreement with it, the more I told myself I was playing the victim and that it wasn't even that bad anyway. The fact that it was my biological father made it all harder. For the years, I had managed to forget the abuse; I had treated him like a real father, like someone who hadn't stolen my innocence.

Only after the buried pain of the years caught up to me did I know that what I had been through was one of the worst things ever. As that happened, the way I viewed and acted towards my father started to change. Before, it was easy to see my father the way I saw him because my brain had totally forgotten that I'd been abused. All that changed when I remembered. I started having animosity and anger as I remembered what had been done to me.

### Tactics the perpetrator uses

Perpetrators use smart tactics to draw in the children and keep them silenced. They know that trust will keep their dark actions a secret. They go above and beyond to seem friendly and non-threatening to the child. This creates a false sense of comfort and security, making it hard for the child to suspect any wrongdoing or to speak out. Pretending to be kind is their only way to manipulate and take advantage for a long time without getting caught.

They tend to be controlling when it comes to the child's life. It's common for them to decide who the child can see or spend time with. They might even refuse to let the child do things, like see friends or be by themselves with others. Eventually, school would be the only place the child can stay alone because they have to. The perpetrator wants to control the child so everything can be kept a secret. Not only have they stolen a valuable thing from the child, but they have also limited the child's freedom.

A second tactic perpetrators often use is to play with the child's curiosity. They know that children are naturally curious, so they try to see how far they can go with the child's curiosity. The predators may play games or watch things to spark a child's curiosity. This creates an environment that makes them more vulnerable to abuse. That's why even if there was no violence, it doesn't mean it wasn't abuse. Your curiosity and your innocence were played with and disrupted. That's the abuse.

### Manipulation

People who have survived abuse often downplay what happened to them, saying things like "It wasn't that bad" or "At least I wasn't beaten." Downplaying their trauma is a way for them to cope, but it hides the deep emotional scars that are still there. When you downplay your experiences to protect yourself, you hold yourself back from healing. If you avoid facing your reality, you might find yourself caught in a cycle of pain that continues. Recognise your pain and what you are going through so you can begin to move forward and heal.

**Pauline's story: Was it really abuse if…?**

All throughout the abuse, my father would do what seemed like loving acts. He would buy me the most expensive clothes and would buy me anything I wanted. He would buy me my favourite snacks. When the abuse stopped, it was hard to put a finger on it. On several occasions, I asked myself if it was really abuse if they were also doing all these loving acts. The loving acts to me seemed to have diluted the abuse. I always felt saying that it was abuse was me being dramatic and becoming a victim. I had moments where I felt like believing it was abuse meant I was just finding a reason to feel sorry for myself. Most abuse stories contain violence. When the abuse you faced didn't involve violence, it can make you doubt whether what happened still counts as abuse.

The predator's tactics make it hard for victims to tell if it was abuse. To a child, the loving acts of the abuser would smother the abuse and make it less severe. The child then finds it hard to distinguish between the tactic and the abuse that was happening to them.

**No violence doesn't mean no abuse**

No violence doesn't mean that it wasn't abusive. Violence isn't what determines whether it was abuse or not. When you think it does, you find it hard to come out and speak about what has been going on behind closed doors. You will wonder: does it count as abuse if violence is the only proof? If you don't see that abuse is abuse without violence, you will often think you are lying to people about it.

For example, if the abuse was also mixed with loving acts. They would struggle to tell the two apart. It complicates things as adults. It's hard to believe it was abuse when the loving acts didn't include any violence.

Violence isn't the only thing which makes behaviour or action abusive. The mere fact that there was no consent makes it abuse. The fact that your innocence was stolen is abuse. If you are unsure if it was abuse it means it was. If it wasn't abuse, it would be clear that it wasn't. But, after years of manipulation and control, it's hard to see it as abuse.

**Abuse v pleasure**

It takes a lot of bravery to speak out about your story. It's harder if you think you could have done something to prevent it. It's common to feel guilty for not stopping the abuse. This is especially true if at times you couldn't tell if it was abuse or pleasure. The guilt eats you as you believe you had the power to stop it but you didn't. Remember, it's important to be kind to yourself. You are not to blame for what happened. And because of how your body sometimes reacted, you may feel like it doesn't count as abuse. You were conditioned to believe it was pleasurable. It's much like a child who laughs at a joke they don't understand because others find it funny.

Many times, you may feel guilty because your body responded in a way that wasn't negative. Remember, the lack of consent and the manipulation to make you believe it wasn't wrong was the abuse. It could have been the case that the perpetrator convinced you that it was a pleasure. Over time, the idea of it being abuse is removed, and now it just looks like pleasure. The guilt may eat you up more, especially when you feel like you knew it wasn't right but still felt some sort of pleasure. Now there's more shame attached to the abuse because you feel like you consented in a way when you didn't. You should know that just because they tricked you into thinking it was pleasure and not abuse, it doesn't mean you consented. That's not what consent is.

Your brain as a child was disrupted and altered, especially with everything you dealt with at such a young age. And because of how your body sometimes reacted, you may feel like it doesn't count as abuse. To ease your guilt, the abuse didn't continue because you wanted it to. The constant manipulation from the perpetrator is what kept it going, not you.

**The power to stop it**

If the abuse did not include violence, you might think you had the power to say no. You may carry this burden of thinking you could have stopped it, but you don't know because you never tried. Thinking of the possibility of what could have happened if you tried leaves you feeling extra guilty. You feel that if you tried, then it would have stopped. There would have been times when you wanted to stop everything by saying no. But, when it came to it, the words didn't come out. It was like your brain froze. It's hard to say no, especially when you have been manipulated consistently. A lot of strength is needed, and it's even harder when the manipulator is someone who should have protected you.

### Comparing what you went through

Comparing your situation to how bad others have it downplays your struggles. It stops you from opening up about your experiences because other people have it way worse. You dismiss your pain to avoid seeming like a victim. You don't want to appear hurt by your past because others have it worse. It's hard to grasp how severe the trauma was. Even after accepting it was abuse, a part of you will feel you didn't go through enough for it to be considered abuse.

But do you see how much it has affected you? You had to live in a pit because of what they did. You are trying to get yourself out of the hell they put you in when they took advantage of you. Your life has never been the same ever since that traumatic experience happened. You lost years to the pain. The abuse cost you a lot. It really did. When you think about all you lost and couldn't have, you'll realise you went through more than enough. You'll see there's no threshold to abuse, no matter how little you think you suffered.

Your life hasn't been the same because of it. How you feel because of what you went through isn't there for no reason. Your wound goes deeper because you went through too much. But with everything you did go through, you never gave up, and you pushed through to the other side. You should be proud of yourself.

**It would be bad if it was someone else so why not when it's you?**

You become very harsh on yourself after a long period of suffering. You start to invalidate how you feel as a way of surviving. You have to tell yourself it's not that bad so you can keep going. And because you have done this for so long, it later becomes hard to believe it really was abuse. Because of this, you don't see it as abuse because it was happening to you, but if it was someone else, it would have been so bad. When it comes to this, you need to realise it's deep. If it were someone else, you would see how bad it is. Some things don't seem that bad when they are in your brain, but once you voice them, it clicks that actually that was very bad. Talking more about the abuse will open your mind. You will then see that it was in fact abuse.

Unintended abuse still counts as abuse. It doesn't matter if you think they weren't being abusive. It still counts as abuse. Even doing something unintentionally doesn't make it less wrong. It doesn't change the fact that their behaviour is their responsibility.

# LIFE AFTER TRAUMA

# Who you used to be

Temptation to go back to your old ways will always be there. In searching for your true identity, it's easy to feel drawn back to what you know. This new life is an unknown territory, so it's normal to miss the habits that once defined you even though they no longer serve you. There will be times you will want to run back to the comfort zones you were hidden in and do the stuff which was easy to do. Remember, growth and change are uncomfortable. That's why not everyone does it. Remind yourself why you wanted to change and what you will gain from being your true self. Finding a way to navigate these changes is necessary to avoid going back. Always remember that even though the journey will sometimes feel lonely, God is by your side even when you don't feel He's there. Even in those times when it feels like He's forgotten and abandoned you, He is right there even in those moments. The Bible says He won't leave you or forsake you. So, believe He won't abandon you in your darkest moments.

### Never look back

Lot's wife in the Bible struggled with the new thing that was happening in her life. For context, the place Lot's family lived in was going to be destroyed because of sexual sin and lawlessness. Before it was destroyed, God warned the family of what was going to happen. He told them, "Don't look back while fleeing the collapsing city." Now, the day for them to run away finally came. Lot's wife didn't listen to what she was told. While fleeing, she looked back at the burning city and consequently turned into a pillar of salt. She was so fixed on her past that she ignored her future, and that cost her life. That's why you shouldn't look back when you are leaving a place that was destroying you. Dwelling on negative memories and emotions can blind you to the present and God's future for you. Looking back can paralyse you and prevent you from embracing the new path God has laid for you. Don't look back as you abandon the places that are draining your energy. Instead, focus on the present. Trust that God is leading you to a brighter, more fulfilling future.

As my faith grew stronger, my world got brighter. God's words changed how I saw myself, and suddenly, I felt more positive and finally belonged somewhere. But weirdly enough, I found myself struggling with this now-happy life I was living. I had lived so many years in a depressive state that I couldn't imagine life outside it. When things finally got better, I found it hard to embrace the good because I wasn't used to it.

To overcome this challenge, I needed to accept my past wasn't the life God intended me to live. The abuse I faced shaped me, but it wouldn't be my forever. Life is hidden in Christ, so when I get to know Him and embrace Him, I will have access to the fullness of what life is. My norm was a depressing life full of sadness, but it doesn't mean that's how it should have been. I had become comfortable with all the negativity that comes with trauma. For a good 5 years, I had been in this dark hole and made it my light. Negative thinking was a lifestyle, but God reminded me that those thoughts don't come from Him. The thoughts God has towards me are pure, and they aren't like the evil ones I had after my painful experience. The closer my relationship with God grew, the more my mental state started to change.

My past was still haunting me, and the enemy was using it to remind me that I was meant to be stuck in the dark. At times, the voice of the enemy sounded louder only because I was paying more attention to it. My past proved that what the enemy was whispering was true, so, of course, I was more drawn to it. But with God by my side, it was different. Even with my pain and feeling like it was getting worse, He promised me that as long as He was with me, life would be better. The hold my childhood had on me started to weaken, and I saw a way forward. I finally knew I wasn't going to be stuck in that gloomy state forever.

As your life becomes better, you may doubt whether you deserve all this happiness. Peace is unsettling for a soul that's always been at war. The struggle is normal, so a life without it feels uneasy like something is missing. But remember, God wants you to live a meaningful life overflowing with purpose, joy and peace. This isn't just a wish but a promise rooted in scripture. God says He "knows the plans he has for you, plans to prosper you and not to harm you, plans to give you hope and a future." A promise that God has a plan for your life regardless of everything you have been through. Your situation doesn't decrease God's power, no matter how big it is. He's beyond capable of creating a beautiful life out of your brokenness. In tough times, when you feel defeated, remember this. What comes after will be greater than the suffering you have endured. There is a brighter future waiting for you, filled with hope and joy.

**Unlearning who you were**

Becoming who God has always seen you to be means that you are going to unlearn who trauma has taught you to be. This process is not easy. It's a struggle to shed the false identity and behaviour patterns trauma has placed on you over time. As you let go of the lies trauma taught you, you will uncover your true self. Surrendering to God's plan for your life gives you a fresh sense of who you are and where you belong. It's like finding the missing piece of a puzzle that finally makes sense of your entire existence.

Healing doesn't always look pretty. It can be messy, painful, and raw. No one prepares you for the constant breakdowns that come with healing. For the times when it is like you're taking two steps forward, then falling three steps back. It's the feeling of being drained and exhausted. Yet having the strength to keep going. Healing is about pushing through the darkness, even when the light at the end of the tunnel seems lost. After years of bottling emotions, a weight lifts as you finally release numbed pain. That's what healing is about—breaking free from the chains of trauma. It's about breaking patterns adopted by trauma and replacing them with healthy ones.

Healing isn't just about becoming happy. It's also about embracing the tears that flow when you admit you're hurt. In fact, it begins with the courage to confront your painful past. Exposure to these wounds will hurt worse than the first time you got hurt. So, allowing yourself to cry and validating your emotions lets you face and deal with how deep those old wounds really are.

Healing doesn't always look like sunshine; it also looks like rain because like a plant, you need both to grow. But even the ugliest moments shape your journey back to wholeness. Surround yourself with the right people. Indulging in things that add to you, not take, and finally being consistent with these things will take you to where you belong.

## Big things vs The small things

Before and after I got baptised, I prayed and asked God to make me happy. I had lived under this dark cloud of depression to the point I had forgotten what happiness looked like. After living a life of misery and pain, happiness was all I wanted to experience. God didn't only make me happy. He did more than I could even think to pray for. He didn't just give me joy but also peace that surpasses all understanding.

As I let Him into my wounded parts, He helped me overcome depression, anxiety and self-hate. God took away all my biggest struggles and I thought my healing journey ended when he did that. For the first time, I wasn't depressed and could see the world from a much brighter perspective.

What I didn't know was that God healing the big parts of me only meant that the smaller, not so-loud wounds were revealed. For once, my brain wasn't in a fog anymore. I could see more clearly now. As the big struggles faded, it became more apparent what other minor things needed to be dealt with. There will always be big and small things that you need to work on. The big things are the ones that run your life, and the little ones rule certain parts of your life. Overcoming the big struggles opens space to see the small things that need change.

**Beating yourself up for feeling the way you used to before**

Healing never meant you wouldn't feel those emotions again. You are still human. It's about knowing and dealing with them in a healthy way. After working hard to get to where you are now, it will sometimes feel like you have made no progress. This will happen when you start to feel like how you did at your lowest. You've been trying your best to heal, and you want everything to work out so you can be happy. Frustration builds up, and happiness feels like it's always out of reach, so you start to beat yourself up.

Give yourself grace for making it this far despite everything you have been through. Every small step forward is a win. You're way more resilient than you think, stronger than you know, braver than you believe. Enjoy the journey, not just the end goal. Keep going - your story isn't finished yet.

You have to always reflect on who you used to be and who you are now; that's where you can see how far you have come. The best way to check your progress is to check your actions. Fair enough you feel the same way you used to, but don't respond the same way you used to. You deal with it so much better; you don't stay in that place for as long as you used to. You don't react the same way when they say the same things they used to say. Your growth is in how you respond. You have come so far; you are amazing and doing amazing. When you feel like you haven't made any progress, look back to where you are coming from.

**It can get lonely**

This journey can get lonely because you will naturally find that you are readjusting. This loneliness is a different type; it's peaceful loneliness. Things you used to enjoy doing just aren't fun anymore. You move on from friendship groups. Old friends might not get you like they used to. It's tough to deal with, but it shows you're really growing. So, embrace the process - it's shaping your authentic self. It's what you need. It's a chance to rebuild and form friendships with like-minded souls. Change hurts but also opens doors to new experiences and getting to know yourself better. Take this chance to make yourself an even better person.

**Grieving what you never had**

Losing your childhood to a traumatic event will haunt you. You will spend some of your adult years grieving your lost childhood. A part of healing from childhood trauma is grieving the life you were not allowed to have. As an adult, you will reflect on the years of your childhood that were stolen. The thoughts of what might have been can feel heavy. So, you mourn your childhood and the life you could have had if you hadn't gone through what you did. Everyone deserves a childhood. There's this longing to be a child again, except for you can't be that anymore. Many years have been wasted, and life just seems to be running past you. Grieving the life you didn't live is confusing, especially when you become an adult. You feel like you missed something, and the thing is… you did miss something. You missed such a key part of your development. Remember that God will restore your locust years with something way better. So, in the years you lost, God will transform your life in a strange and wonderful way. He will give you more than what you lost. God has a strange way of returning what you lost. He also gives you what you never knew you could have. He blesses you in a wonderful way that doesn't make sense.

Grieving your childhood is one thing. But grieving a lost bond with the person who was supposed to protect you is another. You dwell on what could have been. You wonder how life would be if that person hadn't done what they did. What makes this grief worse is if you innocently loved this person, but they ended up hurting you. There's this growing fantasy you have of who the person could have been. Dwelling on unfulfilled potential makes the grief last longer. You dwell on who they could have been, not who they were. That's what keeps you missing them and even feeling sorry for them.

Longing for a relationship with an idolised version of them will cloud your reality of them. Taking them for the person they showed you to be will ease your heartache. You grieve harder when you imagine them as someone they weren't to you.

**Building backup**

You will be tearing down and building back up a lot. While you no longer struggle with the things you used to, it's still hard to adjust to your new life sometimes. Things will have changed so much that you will lose some people in the process of finding you. Some relationships in your life only lasted because the old version of you suited them. Now, people won't like the fact that you are starting to know your worth. They are unhappy that they can't cross over the boundaries you have set. They aren't happy because they can't use you like they used to.

Now they don't know how to go about this new you, so the relationship is going to break down. When you lose people like this, never count it as a loss because them leaving you is doing you a big favour. These aren't people you needed to go with you on this journey. So, while it seems like a loss at the moment, it's a blessing. What you saw as a loss, God saw as a distraction. He did you a favour and removed those people you wouldn't have had the courage to cut off yourself. Not everyone who was there before needs to be with you after. Some people are lessons, like the people you lose.

Some are blessings, like those you meet who encourage your growth after trauma.

Your new friendships will matter, unlike your past ones. They won't be based on how others could benefit from you. Your new friends will value you for who you are. They stay because they like you. They can't imagine life without you, so stay with those people. You have made it this far, so don't drag the people who you couldn't take. They were left behind for a reason.

# Better Days Are Coming

God created you with the unique ability to adapt and change. Trauma doesn't have to control your life because you can grow and become better from it. There is hope that your worst experiences can be used to turn your life into something beautiful. Even with your biggest insecurities, you will one day be able to love yourself for who you are.

One day, you will embrace yourself despite everything you have been through. The guilt will leave you, and what you went through won't look like your fault anymore. The grass still remains greener where you are. You weren't able to see it, not because you didn't water it but because someone dumped mud all over it.

The light isn't on the other side of the tunnel, but it's with you as you walk through the tunnel. When you are blinded, you won't see the light. But, as you heal, you will find beauty in the life which was hidden by trauma. You will see the light has been with you all along. So, even if you don't see it right now, find comfort in knowing that it is there. Once you come out of your dark place, you will realise that you weren't walking alone. One day, you'll reach the other side. You'll see you didn't get there by yourself. A light was guiding you through it.

**You're not you when you are depressed**

What you went through changed everything about you. It's hard to imagine being anyone but who you are now. But remember, you were created to grow, rebuild, and destroy. You were created to grow past your trauma, rebuild what was selfishly stolen, and destroy the image they created for you. The best thing is that you will never have to rebuild alone. God sits and walks beside you, even when you can't see or feel Him.

Trauma created this version of you, which blurred who you really are. It doesn't mean you lost your identity; it just means that it's hidden below all the pile of trauma. When you are depressed, the version of you then isn't who you really are. During this period of depression, the way your mind is shaped doesn't reflect the true reality. But once God fills you up with His peace, you will start seeing who you truly are. Once you come out of depression, you will look back at who you were and be shocked at the life you lived before. You'll be amazed at how different you are when you're no longer depressed. The change will be drastic, making your old self unrecognisable.

**Don't wait till it's unbearable**

Don't wait until everything gets chaotic and helpless before seeking God's help. I waited until everything got unbearable before deciding that I wanted a change. I endured a lot of things which could have been easily avoided if I treated my healing as urgent. If you can avoid getting to a point where everything seems impossible, then do so. If you've tried everything and are running on empty, rest on the fact that God can fill you up again. There will be many things you will have to unlearn. There are habits you are going to have to change. But, while unlearning old habits, new ones start to develop. These characteristics are what's going to make you who God intended for you to be.

**Your scars are evidence that you were once hurting but now you are healed.**

Your scars tell a story. They are the proof that you were once hurting, but now you are healed. God will meet you at your brokenness, and He will turn the pain into joy. To get to the point where you are redeemed, you need not be comfortable in your pain and suffering. Stop sympathising with the enemy's work in your life. Instead, let God show you what He can do in your life. There's a version of you that already exists inside you. Keep being persistent in seeking healing from God, and that version will come to life.

**God's plan for you**

Surrender your life to Jesus and understand that you can't do this journey by yourself. Some days, you'll feel weak and defeated. You'll feel like you can't do it and want to give up. It's in these times that God's strength is made perfect. He keeps you going even when you are ready to throw in the towel. So, you can rely on God entirely. Even in your worst times, His goodness is still evident. When you are crushed, you might doubt God's plan for you. But this dark, broken season won't last forever. The Bible reassures you. It says, "Weeping may endure for a night, but joy comes in the morning." This means that when you have lived broken and bruised, God will always restore your joy even after all that. When you let God into those pain places, your brokenness turns into wholeness. Let me tell you one thing: you will never regret letting God into your life. Give Him a chance with your past, and He will show you a new life. The grass is already greener on your side; it's just been mixed with weeds and litter. Once all the gardening and the cleaning are finished, you will see that your grass has always been greener.

**The small idea you have of God**

The effect of any abuse is detrimental and life-changing. Having bad experiences throughout your life can limit how you see God. Your view of God can be belittled. Trusting and obeying God while He shows up for you during this time will help you see how powerful He really is. He has the ability to take away the dark cloud and fill those empty parts of you. He will change the opinion you have towards yourself and show you your true identity. Despite what you have gone through, trauma does not define you. Be comforted that there is still life after trauma. God turns all the ugly, messy things in your life into beauty. He turns the mess into a message. He is the author of your life. Each day, give Him a chance to show you what each chapter of your life so far means. He will restore you from the heartbreak, trauma, and grief each chapter of your life has brought.

Some experiences blur your true self. Discovering the person you are becomes harder when you don't know who you are supposed to be. I know life may have distorted you. It may have messed with your self-image. I want you to find comfort in this: If you get to know your creator, you will know yourself.

I can't imagine the pain, pressure, and urge to escape. But trust that God works things for your good. It took six years for me to really see that it does get better, but God kept saying the same thing to me through the journey. He kept saying, 'Trust me and my word. The same goes for you. God sees you. Keep going with the hope that God has already worked it out.

### Feel to heal

Being sad about your current circumstances doesn't make you look like you don't have faith that it will get better. Jesus knew that he was going to raise Lazarus from his death, but he still cried before he did it.

You can know it's going to get better, but still be upset about the circumstances that you are currently in. Knowing that better times are ahead doesn't mean what's happening now doesn't hurt. Acknowledging that things will get better eventually doesn't dismiss current struggles. It's valid to feel distressed by immediate hardships. What's happening right now still matters, even with knowing it can't compare to what's to come. Feel your frustrations. This moment's hardships won't last forever, but they're real now. It's normal to get frustrated when progress feels slow. Better times are ahead, even if they're unseen.

### It can't stay like this forever

Change normally starts when you decide that enough is enough. It begins when you decide you do not want life as it is. When you get to this point, it means you have endured a lot. At this point, you are desperate for change. But to get to the point where your brokenness turns into wholeness, you need to not settle.

Those depressing mornings will be bright one day. You will wake up feeling better each day because you didn't settle. The previous pages of your life's story have been dull and horrific, but now it's time to rewrite the rest of the book. Your inner strength can only carry you so far; that's why you need to let go and allow God to step in. At that enough-is-enough phase, you let God do His wonders and change your life completely. It will help you heal from past emotional trauma. It will turn your wounds into scars. They will remind you of your struggles. But they will also prove you survived and are now thriving.

**Consistency= break through**

Once you have gotten to the point where you have decided to work in partnership with God, consistency is key. With consistency comes a breakthrough. There are many things you gain from being consistent. You become more disciplined. You train your mind not to quit when things get tough.

It's time you took your crown back. You have been through so much. There has been so much heartbreak that it feels like that's all there is in life. Even in the midst of all the sadness, a glimmer of hope remains - a gentle voice that promises better days ahead. Although the grief of a lost childhood clouds your view right now, keep this in mind: this too will pass. Just like seasons, winter will give way to spring's renewal, and before long, the warmth of summer will be back.

## From P

Seasons change as evidence that nothing ever stays the same. One day the chilly winter will give way to summers warmth. Even with trauma there's still a beautiful life on the other side. Your scars will soon be evidence that you went through something but are now healed.

Thank you for coming on this journey with me. I hope this book gives you hope that you can overcome too.

# About the author

Many women have unfortunately suffered the consequences of someone else's selfish actions. It is my desire that they find hope in knowing even with everything they have been through there's still life after trauma.

Pauline founded DiscoverrHerr in 2024. After overcoming the struggles of her childhood experiences, she knew more had to be done. Discoverrherr is dedicated to helping women discover who they are past their trauma. Its aim is to guide women to find an identity that's worth keeping.

Find me on
Instagram @discoverrherr
Tiktok @discoverrherr

Visit out wesbite for More information : Discoverrherr.com

Made in the USA
Monee, IL
16 September 2026

63035029R00166